SHAKTI GAWAIN

Specific meditations and step-by-step exercises to help you:
■ Uncover your unconscious beliefs ■ Untangle your feelings ■ Discover your Higher Power ■ Become a creative channel ■ Recognize the voice of intuition ■ Learn from the world around you ■ Risk doing what you want

LIVING IN THE LIGHT WORKBOOK

A Guide to Personal and Planetary Transformation

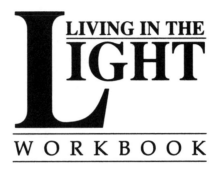

LLIVING IN THE IGHT

WORKBOOK

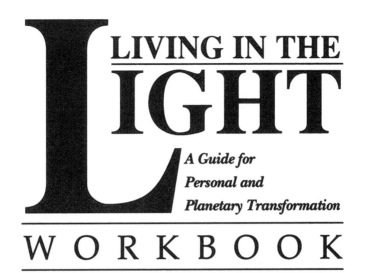

LIVING IN THE LIGHT

*A Guide for
Personal and
Planetary Transformation*

WORKBOOK

SHAKTI GAWAIN

NATARAJ
PUBLISHING

Published by
Nataraj Publishing
P.O. Box 2430
Mill Valley, CA 94942

Cover design: Katheen Vande Kieft

Text design: Cassandra Chu

Word processing: Deborah Eaglebarger

The author of this book does not dispense medical advice nor prescribe the use of any technique as a form of treatment for physical or mental problems without the advice of a physician either directly or indirectly. In the event you use any of the information in this book neither the author nor the publisher can assume any responsibility for your actions. The intent of the author is only to offer information of a general nature to help you in your quest for personal growth.

ISBN 1-882591-02-X

First Printing, May 1991
Fourth Printing, September 1996

Printed in the USA

10 9 8 7 6 5 4

ACKNOWLEDGEMENTS

I'd like to acknowledge Laurel King, who created the first draft of this manuscript and a majority of the exercises.

I'd like to thank Leslie Keenan for helping with the finishing touches.

Thanks to Kathy Altman for contributing some exercises and good ideas.

And thanks to Marc Allen without whom (as usual) this book would not have happened. . . .

TABLE OF CONTENTS

INTRODUCTION   9

    How to Use the Workbook   11

THE FOUNDATION   13

    The Higher Power Within You   15
    Intuition   21
    Becoming a Creative Channel   35
    Spirit and Form   41

THE WORLD AS OUR MIRROR   45

    Mirroring   47
    The Male and Female Within   63
    Tyrant and Rebel   69
    Victim and Rescuer   75

FEELINGS   83

DAILY LIFE   89

    Money   91
    Work and Play   97
    Health   103
    Your Perfect Body   111
    Relationships   123
    Sexuality and Passion   131
    Our Children   139

LIFE AND DEATH   147

A NEW WAY OF LIFE   151

MAKING CHANGE   159

WORKSHOP INFORMATION   163

INTRODUCTION

In my book *Living in the Light: A Guide to Personal and Planetary Transformation* I describe a challenge that I believe we human beings are facing at this point in the evolution of consciousness here on earth. The challenge is for each of us as individuals to reconnect with our deepest spiritual source and learn to live moment to moment, day by day in accordance with the guidance of our own inner sense of truth. In order to do this, we must develop the ability to listen to and follow our intuition — that deep inner guidance that we all have but most of us have learned to ignore.

With a little support and practice, most people can begin to connect with and trust their intuitive sense. As we learn to follow our inner guidance, it can lead us step by step in very practical ways to solve problems, dissolve limitation, and expand creativity in every area of our lives — health and well-being, relationships, career and finances, emotional healing, and spiritual development. The more we are able to trust ourselves and follow our inner truth, the richer and more fulfilled our lives become. And I believe that it is only through this type of individual personal commitment to a life of integrity and balance that we can heal and transform our world.

This workbook has been designed as an accompaniment or follow-up to *Living in the Light*. Modifications have been made on the order of some sections to make this a useable workbook. A few of the meditations and exercises from *Living in the Light* have been included in this book, but for the most part they are new and different. The purpose of this workbook is to assist you in exploring more fully, deeply, and specifically how these ideas and principles can be applied usefully in your own life.

I recommend that, if possible, you read *Living in the Light* and do the meditations and exercises in that book before beginning this

---

workbook. In some cases, however, that may not be necessary; you may find the workbook useful and valuable on its own. Trust your intuition about this!

I sincerely hope that this workbook will be a useful tool for you, and that you find it creative and fun as well.

With love,
Shakti

HOW TO USE THE WORKBOOK

Each chapter of the workbook starts with a few introductory paragraphs followed by an exercise or a series of exercises. Some exercises are meditations; many of them involve writing or, occasionally, drawing. There is room to write and draw in the workbook itself (there's even extra space in the margins for notes). However, you may find that you desire or require more room than given. If so, I suggest that you get a separate notebook and use all the space you need. You might want to use it as a journal of the process you go through while you are working on this material, recording your dreams, daily thoughts, feelings, and insights. You might also like to keep the workbook and refer back to it later, or go back and redo certain exercises at another time. The book has been designed with plenty of space so that you can use it more than once.

I also suggest that you equip yourself with wonderful colored pens, pencils, and/or crayons and experiment with different ways of using them with this material. Go ahead and play with your creativity! After all, no one else ever needs to see what you do, unless you choose to show someone.

Since the workbook starts with the basic principles and builds on that foundation, you may wish to do most of the exercises in the order given. But if you desire, you can work only on the sections that attract you, or you can skip around. Some of you may take a few weeks to work through this material; others may experience a process that could extend over a few years! Trust your own process and do what feels right for you.

Some of you may find it beneficial to form a support group with a few friends and meet weekly or monthly, doing the exercises together and sharing your feelings and responses to the changes, challenges, and miracles you will be experiencing in your lives.

One very important note: The material in this workbook touches into some very profound areas in the psyche and may bring up lots of emotions and feelings. It can be very important and helpful to have professional support from a good therapist in working through these feelings and issues — either in individual counseling or in a group setting. I am a great believer in therapy. I feel that most people on a path of consciousness need the insight offered by a professional therapist at certain times. Be sure to find one who feels truly supportive and trustworthy. Don't be afraid to interview several until you find someone with whom you feel comfortable. If you feel you can't afford professional therapy, alternatives for emotional support could include twelve-step programs such as Alcoholics Anonymous, Overeaters Anonymous, Al-Anon, Codependents Anonymous, Debtors Anonymous, and so on. The meetings are free and are available in most cities.

I wish you increasing energy, awareness, joy, creativity, prosperity, and aliveness as you continue your journey of discovery.

Love and light,
Shakti

THE FOUNDATION

The basic principles described in *Living in the Light*, which we will be exploring here, are these:

- You have a Higher Power within you.
- You can learn to listen to your Higher Power through your intuitive guidance.
- You are a spiritual being contained in physical form.
- You are a channel for the creative energy of the universe to come into the physical world.

By learning to follow your own intuitive guidance, you can bring your physical life increasingly into alignment with your spiritual being. As you bring your individual life into balance and integration you contribute greatly to the transformation of the world.

The exercises that follow will help define and clarify what these words mean to you. Each individual is unique. Therefore, each of you will experience your higher power, intuition, channeling, spirit and form in your own way. If your experiences differ from those of others, this is not an invalidation of the experience, but rather a celebration of your unique being. I hope you will enjoy your journey of discovery as you build your own foundation.

THE HIGHER POWER WITHIN YOU

The foundation for life in the new world begins with the understanding that there is a higher intelligence, a fundamental creative power or energy in the universe, which is the source and substance of all existence. Some of the words used to describe this intelligence are:

God	I Am
Spirit	The Force
Higher Power	Source
The Light	Cosmic Intelligence
The Universe	Inner Guidance
Higher Self	Christ Consciousness

This workbook begins with discovering your relationship with this Higher Power. Do you believe in this intelligence, or are you unsure of its existence? If you believe in it, are you willing to trust this power? If you are uncertain, are you willing to take a leap of faith and simply act as if you believe in it for a period of time to see what you experience?

Once we acknowledge this power within us and learn to trust it, we can open up to receiving guidance in our lives. Though this guidance may come in many forms, some unexpected or even unusual, it will eventually lead to increased joy, health, energy, and prosperity.

As we learn to trust in the Higher Power of the universe absolutely, we will begin to live in accordance with universal principles. We can then enjoy the more abundant, creative, healthy, and fulfilling lives that await us.

EXERCISE 1

To trust a Higher Power completely it is essential to have a concept of that Higher Power as trustworthy. Since we are human, we tend to attribute human qualities to that Higher Power, and sometimes the qualities we attribute are *not* ones that build trust.

People's concepts of God usually stem from the past. They are based on early religious training and/or family experiences. For many people a Higher Power means an authority figure or parent that guided them as children. So if the adults around them were powerful and loving or critical and punishing, then those were the qualities they would attribute to God. For others, God is something they read about and learned about in church or from those around them. For most it is a combination of concepts they've picked up from others, not an experience they've felt within themselves.

With this in mind, the following questions can help clarify and expand your vision of this intelligence and your relationship to it. In answering these questions write down the first things that come to your mind. If you find yourself struggling, let go of the question and move on to the next.

A. In the space below list ten qualities of the God you learned about as a child. For example:

1. *frightening*   3. *powerful*
2. *big*   4. *judgmental*

1.   2.

3.   4.

5.   6.

7.   8.

9.   10.

Are these qualities trustworthy?

B. If your belief in a Higher Intelligence has changed since child-hood and you now see or feel it differently, list ten qualities that you now attribute to this force. For example:

1. energy source
2. loving
3. omnipotent

1.   2.

3.   4.

5.   6.

7.   8.

9.   10.

C. If you were to expand your belief in a Higher Power even fur-ther so that you totally trusted it at all times, what qualities would that power have? For example:

1. totally reliable
2. all-knowing
3. offers total acceptance

1.   2.

3.   4.

5.   6.

7.   8.

9.   10.

D. Close your eyes. As you inhale imagine you are breathing into your body all the positive qualities of that power; as you exhale let go of and release any qualities unlike this. For example, feel yourself breathing in light, knowledge, acceptance, love, strength, and energy, and as you exhale breathe out tiredness, tension, self-hatred, worry, etc.

EXERCISE 2

To describe your Higher Power further, and to better understand your relationship with it, explore the following questions.

A. Describe briefly what this power looks or feels like. Does it have a human, animal, or light form, or is it a presence or energy? Is it masculine or feminine in nature, or a combination of the two, or neither?

B. What is your relationship with this power? Can you describe how and when you make contact with it? Do you contact this power in a particular physical location (church, temple, or other sacred place), through contact with nature, through meditation or prayer, dance, exercise, etc.? Do you feel this contact in your body, mind, emotions or spirit, or a combination of two or more of these levels?

C. If your relationship to your Higher Power were to grow and expand, what would you desire it to be like? For example, would you like to be in more consistent contact or would you like more specific guidance? Let yourself explore this ideal relationship.

D. Close your eyes and spend a few minutes visualizing that power, presence, or being with you now. Imagine yourself having the kind of relationship you've always wanted with this force — feel, see, and experience it as real right now.

INTUITION

Our Higher Power speaks to us through our intuition. Your intuition is the "gut" feeling within you — the source of your deepest personal truth. If you are willing to listen carefully to this feeling, it will guide you through each step of your life journey. The wisdom of the universe is completely available to us. We only need to learn to listen within to attain it.

How do we get in touch with our intuition? There is no single answer to that question. The process is different for everyone. Some people listen for their intuitive guidance through formal meditation, others through their art, dance, sports, music, writing, walks through nature, or moments of stillness. Your intuition may actually come to you as an inner voice, or you may be guided by a strong feeling or hunch, an image, or an inner sound or vibration.

The following exercises will guide you in contacting your intuition and help you to recognize it clearly. The exercises also may help you realize that you're already in contact with your intuition.

EXERCISE 3

Sit or lie down in a comfortable position in a quiet place. Close your eyes and relax. Take several slow, deep breaths, relaxing your body more with each breath. Relax your mind and let your thoughts drift, but don't hold onto any thought. Imagine that your mind becomes as quiet as a peaceful lake.

Now focus your conscious awareness in to a deep place in your body, in the area of your stomach or solar plexus. It should be the place in your body where you feel that your "gut feelings" reside. This is the physical place where you can most easily contact your intuition.

Imagine that you have a wise being living inside there. You might have an image of what this wise being looks like, or you might just sense that it is there. This wise being is really a part of you — your intuitive self. You can communicate with it by talking to it silently, making requests, or asking questions. Then relax, don't think too hard, and be open to receiving the answers. The answers may come in words or in feelings or images. The answers are usually very simple, they relate to the present moment (not the past or future), and they "feel right." If you don't receive an immediate answer, let go and go about your life. The answer will come later, either from inside of you in the form of a feeling or idea, or from outside through a person, a book, an event, or whatever.

For example, you might say, "Intuition, tell me what I need to know here. What do I need to do in this situation?"

Trust the feeling that you get and act on it. If it is truly your intuition, you will find that it leads to a feeling of greater aliveness and power, and more opportunities begin to open up for you. If it doesn't seem right, you may not have been truly acting from your intuition but from an ego voice in you. Go back and ask for clarification.

It takes practice to hear and trust your intuition. The more you do it, the easier it will become. Eventually you will be able to contact your intuition, ask yourself questions, and know that in that "wise being" within you, an incredible source of power and strength is available to answer your questions and guide you. As you grow more sensitive to this guidance from the intuitive feelings within, you will gain a sense of knowing what you need to do in any situation. Your intuitive power is always available to guide you whenever you need it. It will open to you as soon as you are willing to trust yourself and your inner knowledge.

EXERCISE 4

Another good way to practice getting in touch with your intuition is through nondominant hand writing.

If you are right-handed, let your right hand represent your conscious, rational mind, and your left hand represent your intuitive mind. (If you're left-handed, reverse it.) Use a different colored pen for each hand.

Write a simple question that is of importance to you with your dominant hand. Then without thinking too much, begin to answer it with your other hand. This may feel difficult. (You'll feel like you're in kindergarten again!) Do it anyway. Continue the dialogue as long as it feels appropriate. You may be surprised at what you learn.

Example:

Right hand: What direction should I go in my life now?
*Left hand: Don't worry where to **go**. Be **here**.*

Right hand: But what about my career?
Left hand: Relax. Don't think so much. It will all work out fine. Stop trying so hard.

One of the difficulties in learning to trust and follow our intuitive "voice" is that we have many different "voices" or energies within us, and often they are all feeling and saying different and contradictory things! This can be quite confusing. With practice and awareness we can learn to distinguish the energy of our intuition from any other. In fact, it usually has its own distinct feeling.

Discovering some of the many other inner voices or sub-personalities within us, however, can be useful and important. If we can become aware of who is "talking" to us or directing us internally, we can begin to have much more consciousness and choice in our lives.*

Practice in listening inside will help you to decipher what your "gut feeling" is telling you and to sort out all the other voices inside of you. As you begin to pay more attention to your internal dialogues, you will become more familiar with the varying qualities of the different "sub-personalities."

For example, you may notice that a certain voice inside of you has a judging, critical quality — it's always pointing out what you did wrong. That is your inner "critic." Another voice might always be telling you what you "should" be doing — that's probably your inner "tyrant" or "pusher."

It's important to notice that your Higher Power, coming through your intuition, never speaks in harsh, judgmental, or tyrannical ways. Its tone is encouraging and supportive, and it usually brings a feeling of aliveness and empowerment or comfort and serenity. Following its guidance will not result in pressure, tension, or self-doubt, but in expanded awareness and energy.

There are an infinite number of different "sub-personalities" within us, and each person has a different configuration. Some common ones that you may come to recognize within yourself might be:

The Perfectionist	The Vulnerable Child
The Critic or Judge	The Playful Child

---

*For more complete information on this fascinating topic, read *Embracing Our Selves* and *Embracing Each Other* by Dr. Hal Stone and Dr. Sidra Winkelman, New World Library, 1989. Or listen to their tapes, available through Delos, Inc., P.O. Box 604, Albion, CA 95410.

The Mother or Father	The Adolescent
The Tyrant or Pusher	The Rebel
The Rational Mind	The Creative Artist
The Rescuer	The Victim
The Spiritual Seeker	The Hedonist

You may discover some of these or others while doing the meditations.

If you give each of these voices a chance to speak, you will then be led more easily to your intuitive voice. This next exercise is designed to help you do that. You may want to do it with a friend so that one of you can read the meditation while the other experiences it. Or you can record it in your own voice and then do the exercise as you play it back.

EXERCISE 5

Sit or lie down in a comfortable position in a quiet place. Close your eyes and relax. Take several slow, deep breaths, relaxing your body more with each breath. Relax your mind and let your thoughts drift away. Try not to attach yourself to any one thought. As each thought comes into your mind, let it go.

Now imagine you are walking down a beautiful spiral staircase . . . descending further and further with each step. When you come to the base of the staircase you find a huge door in front of you. Open it up and walk into a large, majestic room with a round table and chairs in it. Take time to explore the room. When you are ready, choose a chair, sit down, and be comfortable. Sit quietly for a while, allowing your mind to become calm and clear. Then gradually start listening for those parts of your personality that want to speak out. When you become aware of one voice as louder than the others, have that part of you take a seat at the table. Let this voice say everything it needs to say. It may be your critical voice that wants to tell you everything you've been doing wrong, or perhaps it's a frightened part of you that wants to describe how frightened he or she is. It may want to talk about one issue or problem in your life, or it may want to discuss your life in general. Let the voice express any thoughts or feelings it has.

As the voice is speaking, other parts of you may begin to react.

For example, while your critical voice has the floor, your rebel or your frightened child may also want to speak. Allow these voices to take a chair, in turn, giving each the opportunity to have a say. The entire table may be filled with different parts of yourself before all opinions and feelings have been expressed. Try not to figure anything out. Just allow the different energies and voices to speak. Take as much time as you need to let each communicate with you. When they have finished speaking, acknowledge each one for what he or she has given you.

After all the voices have spoken, take a few minutes to observe them and acknowledge them as the many parts of your personality. When you feel ready, prepare yourself to move into a deeper level of your being. Imagine yourself leaving the table and walking toward a tunnel. As you enter the tunnel you notice that it is lighted by a beautiful light. As you walk through this tunnel, you absorb this healing light and become aware that the voices grow fainter behind you. This is a magical tunnel that is leading you to a safe, beautiful place. With each step, you get nearer to your inner sanctuary. Soon the tunnel opens up and you are there. What does your sanctuary look and feel like? Create it exactly the way you want it, indoors or outdoors, a place you've been before, or a place you make up right now.

Find a comfortable place to sit or lie down in your sanctuary and breathe deeply until you are relaxed and at peace.

Now focus your conscious awareness on the deep place in your body where your inner being or Higher Power resides. Let your Intuitive Self come forward. Does it have anything to tell you — a message for you? Feel free to talk to your intuition, to make requests or ask questions. Is there anything you want to ask your intuition right now? Ask and relax. Keep your mind free of thoughts and open to receiving the answers. Spend as much time as you want with your intuition. Then, when you are ready, thank your intuition for guidance. Imagine another tunnel that leads you out of your inner sanctuary and back into the room you presently are in. When you come back to the room, slowly become aware of the sounds around you, your feet or body on the ground, and the feeling of the room. Whenever you're ready, simply open your eyes.

In the space below, you may want to record the various voices you experienced and summarize the feelings or ideas each one expressed. Now, describe your inner sanctuary and your experience with contacting your intuition. What was the basic feeling or message you got?

EXERCISE 6

A. Go back in your mind and remember all the times you have gone against yourself — when you have not heeded the guidance of your intuition. List as many of these instances as you can in the space below. What were the results?

Examples:

1. *My intuition kept telling me to quit my job as a counselor and I wouldn't listen.*
   Result: My car broke down three times in one month on the way to work. I felt extremely stressed and had a very hard time dealing with my clients.

2. *My intuition told me to slow down and stop working so hard but fear of financial insecurity caused me to keep pushing myself.*
   Result: I ended up spraining my back and couldn't get out of bed for two weeks.

3. *I felt I should approach my boss with doubts I had concerning risks the company was taking, but I didn't act on this.*
   Result: The company went ahead with its plans and lost a large sum of money.

1.

2.

3.

4.

5.

6.

7.

B. Now, recall all the times you have followed your intuition. List as many of them as possible in the space below, and tell how it felt. What were the results?

Examples:

1. *My intuition told me to sign up for an interior design class.*
   Result: I loved it and am now working part-time at a design center.

2. *I felt my husband and I might have to separate unless we learned to communicate more openly, so we started seeing a counselor.*
   Result: My husband and I are beginning to open up in new ways. We are less dependent on each other and are building a new relationship based on trust and communication.

3. *I had a strong impulse to approach my boss with a creative idea.*
   Result: He was impressed and encouraged me to explore it further.

4. *I decided to quit my nine-to-five job, work part-time, and trust I would earn enough from my consulting work.*
   Result: I now have much more energy and feel good about what I'm doing.

1.

2.

3.

4.

5.

6.

7.

8.

9.

10.

C. Make a list of things you would do today if you totally trusted your intuition. What is your "gut feeling" telling you to do? Learning to trust your intuition is learning to stay in the moment. What would you do right now?

Examples:

1. *Talk to my boss about possible improvements that could be implemented in the business.*
2. *Relax more and stop trying so hard.*
3. *Call the friend I haven't seen in ages and see how he is.*
4. *Arrange to spend a day in the country to enjoy the inspiration from nature.*
5. *Join a support group to help me with the personal issues I'm dealing with.*
6. *Take the afternoon off and take a walk.*
7. *Spend the evening at home instead of going out.*
8. *Sign up for that class I've been curious about.*

1.

2.

3.

4.

5.

6.

7.

8.

9.

10.

BECOMING A CREATIVE CHANNEL

When we surrender fully to the universe within us by listening to and trusting our intuition, we become channels for the creative energy of the universe. (I do not use the term "channel" in the way that is currently popular, meaning a trance medium who channels another entity.) To be a creative channel is to be fully and freely yourself and to know that the universe speaks through you and your creative actions. The more you trust your intuition the stronger and clearer your channel will become. When you willingly follow your intuition, your Higher Power will be channeled through you to manifest its creative work.

Every creative genius has been a channel, and every masterpiece has been created through the channeling process. Great works are never created only by the personality: They arise from a deep, universal inspiration and are given form through the individual ego and personality.

All of us are geniuses — each in our own unique way. But the nature of our individual genius is often hidden from us, buried under our efforts to conform to a reality that does not suit us. As long as we accept others' ideas of how we should live our lives, we will fail to hear the voice of our higher power, and our genius will remain an untapped potential within us. It is only when we listen to our inner voice and trust its guidance that we can learn to be ourselves and to allow our natural channel to open.

EXERCISE 7

To become a creative channel you must risk being who you really are. This may feel like a risk because your true nature may not fit any prior pictures or images you had of yourself. This exercise can help you relax your expectations and allow you a glimpse of your true inner being.

Close your eyes and take a few deep breaths. Ask your intuition to show you an image of your essential self. Accept any image that comes forward. The image may come in a human form or it may be a color, an object, or animal. Regardless of the form, there is a message in whatever picture you will receive. If the significance of the image is not obvious, ask for clarification of the message. Be patient. The message may be immediately clear, or it may be revealed at some later time. If you repeat this exercise at later times you may get different images, and each one will show you some aspect of yourself.

Describe your image in the space below, either in words or in pictures.

EXERCISE 8

To become a creative channel, you must risk doing what you really want.

In Column 1 list all the things you really love to do that you are currently doing.

In Column 2 list things you consistently do even though you don't want to do them.

In Column 3 list everything that you want to do but are not doing.

COLUMN 1	COLUMN 2	COLUMN 3
Things I love that I do	*Things I don't want to do*	*Things I love that I don't do*

Examples:

1. Bicycling
2. Spending time with friends
3. Dancing
4. Cooking
5. Running

Housecleaning

Making business calls

Listening to my sister's concepts about her life

Driving the kids to school

Traveling

Gardening

Playing the piano

Working more with people

1.

2.

3.

4.

5.

6.

COLUMN 1	COLUMN 2	COLUMN 3
Things I love that I do	*Things I don't want to do*	*Things I love that I don't do*

7.

8.

9.

10.

After completing your lists, think creatively about the things you don't enjoy: Are there other ways they could be handled? For example, could you delegate more to other people, hire someone to assist you, or trade with someone who is willing to do an exchange for something you can do? You might also try to organize the unpleasant things differently so that they're easier to do, or spend one hour a day or one day a week doing what you least enjoy and then reward yourself with something you enjoy most. Are there some things you could just stop doing? By reviewing the list creatively, you can consider new options without immediately assuming that options are impossible.

Now apply this process to the other two lists: Can you start doing more of what you love, especially the things you aren't now doing? Start with small steps — take a few minutes a day, or an hour a week for something you want to do, or enroll in a class, or put aside a weekend for something special and different. Write down some ideas and make some specific plans in the space below.

SPIRIT AND FORM

Our spirit is the creative energy of the universe which moves through us to manifest in the world. Our form is our physical body, our mind, and our personality — the medium through which our spirit moves. Although neither spirit nor form could exist apart from one another in this physical world, until we learn to listen to and trust our intuition, our spirit and form will often conflict. While our spirit yearns for greater life, energy, change, and inner fulfillment, our form seeks safety and security and fears risk or change.

As young children, the channels between our spirit and form are relatively open, but as we grow older and learn to shun our intuitive awareness (spirit) in favor of more conventional behavior that conforms to the world around us (form), these channels become blocked. We lose touch with our spirit and forget our purpose for being here. We lose sight of the creative goals and spiritual ideals that come from our spirit. Form becomes paramount, yet our spirit still seeks expression. Thus, we feel dissatisfied and out of balance.

Even though we may enjoy some amount of material success, we are still not happy. In an effort to restore this imbalance we urgently seek gratification — through greater material success, or superficial relationships, or even through various means of escape such as drugs or alcohol. But because we don't understand the true cause of our dissatisfaction — our lack of connection to our spirit — all of our efforts fail. Gradually we succumb to hopelessness.

Yet in this very hopelessness lies our greatest hope, for when we are hopeless we give up — we give up our attachment to the way we've been doing things, and release old behaviors and old forms from our lives. At this point, the channel to our spirit can be reopened, *if* we are guided to listen for the voice of our spirit, our intuition. Our spirit, with all its creative energy and intense drive, is waiting to fill the void in our lives, to provide us with the satisfaction and balance we have been seeking so desperately.

The following exercise helps reveal the distance and degree of conflict between form and spirit that now exist in you and suggests actions you can take to bring your form and spirit into alignment.

EXERCISE 9

In the first column below, list several examples of consistent fantasies you have about things you want to do, how you want to live, or ways you want to express yourself. In the next column, describe what your form is actually doing in relation to this. In the third column, create a step you can take now to respond to and support your spirit through your form. For some of you this may entail taking a physical step into the world, such as following a job lead, trying out for a part in a play, or writing affirmations. For others this step could be lying in bed, meditating, and learning to love and nurture yourself.

SPIRIT	FORM	ACTION
What I desire to do:	What I am now doing:	A step I can take toward expressing my desire:

Examples:

1. Write a novel	I'm now working as a copy editor at a local paper	Begin writing creatively one hour a week just for fun
2. Live in a beautiful, secluded home by the water	I'm living in a dumpy apartment in the city	Talk to a friend about sharing expenses for a more pleasant apartment with a nice yard. A step in the right direction
3. Wake people up about the importance of environmental/ecological issues	Nothing	Join an environmental activist group and pledge a few hours or a few dollars a month toward helping

1.

2.

SPIRIT	FORM	ACTION
What I desire to do:	*What I am now doing:*	*A step I can take toward expressing my desire:*

3.

4.

5.

6.

7.

8.

9.

10.

THE WORLD AS OUR MIRROR

If we understand the metaphysical concept that we each "create our own reality," the external world can serve as a giant mirror which clearly reflects what we believe about ourselves and others. Viewed in this way, the external world can teach us about aspects of ourselves that we can't see directly. Our inner beliefs are reflected outside us, so if you want to know how you feel and what you believe, look around. Just as an artist studies his latest creation to see what works well and what doesn't, we can examine the ongoing masterwork of our lives to appreciate who we are and recognize what we still need to learn.

Life becomes a creative enterprise when viewed from this perspective. We can learn from the reflection of our lives. We can use that information to heal old emotional wounds and core beliefs that keep us stuck in the same limiting or self-defeating patterns. As we become conscious of and release old behavior patterns, we automatically create more balance, harmony, abundance, and fulfillment in our lives.

Those newly introduced to the concept of mirroring may often see something mirrored in their life they don't like and then blame themselves. If you find yourself reacting this way, remember that the universe does not offer us a tool of enlightenment so we can beat ourselves with it. Treat yourself with love and compassion, as you would a child who is eager to learn.

The most important key in changing the outside world is understanding *how* what we feel and believe is reflected outside us. Once we shed light on a process that has been unconscious, it will no longer run our lives without our knowledge. We will regain the power over what happens to us.

MIRRORING

The following exercises on mirroring are intended to help you uncover your unconscious beliefs and guide you in learning to treat yourself better. As you complete the exercises, you will begin to see clearly the changes you have made reflected in the world around you.

Remember, in using the mirroring process it's important to:

1. Assume that everything in your life is your reflection, your creation. No accidents or events are unrelated to you; and

2. Avoid putting yourself down for the reflections you see. Nothing is negative; every reflection is a gift that brings awareness. After all, we are here to learn. If we were already perfect, we wouldn't need to be here.

EXERCISE 10

Focus on a particular incident in your life that is troubling you. In the space below, briefly describe the problem. Then ask yourself how this mirrors how you feel about yourself. Write down the response. Some examples follow. (There is space for you to focus on other incidents later, if you'd like.)

1. *Problem: My boss criticizes any new ideas I have. He seems opposed to innovative ideas.*
   Mirror: I always doubt any new ideas I have. I tell myself they're not good enough. I'm afraid of change.

2. *Problem: One of my closest friends said she felt I had no time for her and that she was a nuisance to me.*
   Mirror: I have no time for myself. I have not valued my feelings and needs lately.

3. *Problem: My boss got angry at me for being late several times this week.*
   Mirror: I have dreaded going into work. I have been angry at myself for continuing to work at a job I hate.

1.

2.

3.

4.

5.

6.

7.

8.

9.

10.

Once you discover how an internal problem actually mirrors what's going on inside of you, try not to blame yourself. Instead, when you realize that something you have been doing to yourself is causing harmful results, ask the universe for help. You can say to your Higher Power "Show me what I need to know about this" or "Help me find consciousness and healing in this part of my life."

EXERCISE 11

We often can see a direct correlation between how we treat ourselves and how others treat us. In the first column, write down all the things you did or said in the last week that were positive or supportive of yourself. Then, in the second column list the ways this self-nurturing was mirrored by positive events. Some examples follow.

WHAT I DID FOR MYSELF

I wrote self-esteem affirmations;
I took a hot bath and meditated;
bought myself a beautiful scarf;
I called Joe to ask about possible
speaking engagements; played
tennis; fixed myself a delicious and
healthy dinner; I asked a co-worker
for help with a project; went
camping with my family; took
myself to my favorite restaurant
for lunch; reorganized my desk and
threw out everything I didn't need;
put flowers on my desk

1.

2.

3.

4.

5.

6.

MIRROR

Two people commented that I looked
beautiful today; found a five-dollar
bill; felt healthy and energetic; got a
letter from my parents with lots of
good news; Bill called and asked me
out; my boss said he liked my work;
got more than I expected in my tax
return; was invited to speak at a
conference in Florida

WHAT I DID FOR MYSELF	*MIRROR*
7.	
8.	
9.	
10.	

EXERCISE 12

Reflect on the different categories of your life — work and career, relationships, money, sexuality and passion, body, home environment. What is the major event or statement that reflects your attitude about each? Write it down in the "mirror" column. Then describe how this reflects your internal belief system in the "belief" column. If you identify a limiting or negative belief, then turn it into an affirmation. Write the affirmation below this negative belief. (There is space for you to add other events later, if you'd like.)

MIRROR	*BELIEF*
Work and Career	
Examples:	
1. *I have a great job that I love to do, but I make a minimal income.*	*I don't believe I can make money doing what I love to do.* **Affirmation:** *I now make a good income doing what I love to do.*

MIRROR	BELIEF
2. *I was fired from my job and I don't know what to do next.*	*I was no longer feeling fulfilled in that job and I wanted to leave but I was afraid to lose the security.* ***Affirmation:** I am being guided step-by-step to work that is right for me.*

1.

2.

3.

4.

MIRROR	*BELIEF*

5.

Relationships

Examples:

1. *I'm always attracted to women who turn out to be emotional and needy.*

    I'm afraid of my own emotions and my need. It would embarrass me to show the vulnerable side of me so I repress it, and the women in my life act it out.
    Affirmation: *It's okay for me to have emotions and needs. It makes me a stronger person to accept my vulnerability. I can share my strength and vulnerability with a strong and vulnerable partner.*

2. *I want a lasting relationship but I can't seem to find someone who wants to make a commitment.*

    I'm afraid to be really committed to myself in a relationship. I always try to please the other person and lose my sense of myself.
    Affirmation: *I am committed to being honest and real in a relationship. I have a strong committed relationship with myself. I am attracting a wonderful partner who is right for me.*

1.

MIRROR   *BELIEF*

2.

3.

4.

5.

| MIRROR | BELIEF |

Money

Examples:

1. *I never have enough money for anything pleasurable or fun, just enough to pay the basic bills.*

   My parents always had just enough. I feel guilty having extra money.
   Affirmation: *It's okay for me to have more money than my parents. It's good for me to have money for pleasure and fun. I deserve to have pleasure in my life. I now have enough money to enjoy myself.*

2. *Money does not come easily.*

   I always have to work hard and really push myself to earn a living. Life is a struggle to survive.
   Affirmation: *Life is fulfilling and enjoyable. Money comes to me easily as I do what I love.*

1.

2.

3.

| MIRROR | BELIEF |
| 4. | |

| 5. | |

Sexuality and Passion

Examples:

1. *I love my wife but I don't have much energy for sex lately. Our sexual relationship seems dull and dead.*

   I'm afraid to express a lot of my feelings and emotions, especially my anger and my fear, for fear my wife will leave me or reject me. I'm deadening myself to a lot of my feelings and my sexual energy reflects that.
   Affirmation: *It's important for me to express my feelings. The more I express my feelings, the more I am loved. I am now expressing my feelings freely and responsibly.*

2. *I only feel passionate around emotionally unavailable men. The others bore me.*

   *My father didn't want me. There must be something wrong with someone who **does**. There must be something wrong with me.*
   Affirmation: *I am now willing to feel passionate about men who want me. I am worth wanting. I deserve to be loved. There's nothing wrong with men who want me. I am attracting wonderful, loving, sexy, emotionally available men into my life.*

MIRROR   *BELIEF*

1.

2.

3.

4.

5.

MIRROR	BELIEF

Body

Examples:

1. *I am overweight and no matter how much I diet I can't seem to keep the weight off.*

   I don't believe I have a right to take up space. I have trouble asserting myself and asking for what I want or setting boundaries with those I love. My body is reacting by taking up the extra "space" that I deny myself emotionally.
   Affirmation: *I have a right to take up space. I ask for what I want. It's okay for me to say "no" to people when I want to. I take care of myself and trust others to take care of themselves. I am a strong, assertive, healthy, slender person.*

2. *I'm tired a lot and I have a lot of minor physical symptoms.*

   I believe that my worth hinges on how much I do, so I push myself all the time to do as much as possible. Resting and relaxing make me feel guilty.
   Affirmation: *I deserve to rest, relax, and nurture myself. My body deserves to be loved and taken care of. Just by being who I am, I am worthy and lovable.*

1.

2.

	MIRROR	BELIEF
3.		
4.		
5.		

Home environment

Examples:

	MIRROR	BELIEF
1.	*My home is too small and cramped. I feel closed in when I'm there.*	*I'm afraid to admit how expansive and powerful I really am and how big my visions are. I'm holding myself back and limiting myself.* **Affirmation:** *I am powerful, creative, and unlimited. I am creating a spacious, attractive home for myself.*
2.	*I want to move but can't find a place at a price I can afford.*	*I don't believe there's a nice place to live within my price range.* **Affirmation:** *I am now living in a wonderful home that I can easily afford.*

	MIRROR		*BELIEF*

1.

2.

3.

4.

5.

Note: As you can see from the examples, our core negative beliefs are often entwined with deep emotional issues. Identifying these beliefs and issues and doing affirmations can be very helpful, but it is *not* a substitute for good professional therapy. I recommend seeking support from a good therapist with experience in the specific issue that is troubling you.

THE MALE AND FEMALE WITHIN

Each of us has male and female energies within us. Our female energy is the intuitive self — the deep, wise, guiding aspect of ourselves. Feminine energy is receptive, thus it forms the channel through which our Higher Self moves to connect with us. Our female speaks to us through inner promptings, gut feelings, or images that arise out of a deep place within us. When we do not listen to the voice of our intuition, the female energy within us will often communicate through dreams or emotions, or through our physical condition.

Our male aspect takes action in the world. It enables us to *do* things — to build, to speak, to move our bodies. Where the female within is receptive, our male energies are assertive, outgoing, and expressive. It is the male within us that brings ideas into being, transforms thought into form.

Female intuition plus male action equal creativity. The feminine is the source of creative inspiration and the masculine implements her vision. The interplay of these energies with us is the vehicle for the creative energy of the universe to channel through us. So the more in tune with each aspect we are, the more easily we are able to listen to and act on the voice of our intuition. In the next few exercises you will meet your inner female and male. They will help you discover your inner goals and visions and make these visions a reality.

In the following meditation, trust the images or feelings that come when you ask to see your inner male and female. One or both could be people you actually know, archetypal or fantasy figures, or in the form of an animal. Accept what comes. If you do the meditation more than once, they may be different each time.

EXERCISE 13

MEDITATION

Sit or lie down in a comfortable position and close your eyes. Take a few deep breaths and allow your body and mind to relax completely. Then gradually move your conscious awareness into a quiet place within you.

Now visualize an image that represents your inner female. This image could be an actual or imaginary person, an animal, or even something abstract such as a color or shape. Accept whatever arises spontaneously in your mind.

Look closely at your female image and try to sense or feel what she represents to you. Notice the image's details, her colors and textures and be aware of how you feel about her.

After you have established a sense of rapport with your female image, ask her if she has anything she would like to say to you right now. Allow yourself to receive her communication in whatever form it may come, whether in words, feelings, or images. If you have any questions for her, ask them. Again, be open to reply in any form.

Once you have received her communication, and you feel complete for the moment, take a deep breath and release her image from your mind. Come back to a quiet, still place.

Now draw to mind an image that represents your male self. Again, accept whatever image comes to you. It could be a man, a boy, an animal, or some abstract symbol or color. Slowly explore this image as well, noting all details, colors, and textures. Become aware of how you feel about him, then ask if he has anything to say to you at this time. Be receptive to his communication, whatever its form. If you have anything you want to ask him, do this now. Accept whatever words, feelings, or images you may receive. If an answer doesn't come to you immediately, know that it will come later.

Once you feel complete with your communication with him, release the male image from your mind and return to a quiet place inside.

Now ask that both your male and female appear to you at the same time. Observe them together. Do they relate to one another or are they separate? If they do relate to one another, how do they relate? Ask them if they have anything they would like to communicate to one another. Stay open to what comes to you in words, images, or feelings. If you have anything you'd like to say to them or ask them, do that now.

When you feel complete, once again take a deep breath and release their images from your mind. Return to a quiet, still place inside before ending this exercise. Take a few deep breaths and open your eyes, feeling refreshed and revitalized. With crayons, paint, or colored pens create a picture of your inner male and fe-male images and/or write about your experiences with them.

EXERCISE 14

MEDITATION

This meditation shows us the power of having a male that supports our female.

Close your eyes and get in touch with your female intuitive voice.

Ask her if she wants anything. Is there a gift she desires or something she wants to say or do? When she has told you what she wants, visualize your new male supporting her desire and taking whatever action is necessary to honor her request.

Be aware of how this feels to you.

EXERCISE 15

In column 1 list everything you (your female) wants and in column 2 list what you (your male) can do to give you (your female) what you want.

In doing this exercise, it's important not to attempt to do too much, otherwise you may begin to feel overwhelmed. Limit your list to one or two things at a time. This will build the trust between your female and male. (There is space for you to come back and add more if you wish.)

FEMALE (What You Want)	MALE (What You Can Do To Give Yourself What You Want)
Examples:	
1. *More rest*	*Put on soft music and lie down for ten minutes.*
2. *Paint*	*Purchase paints and canvas, and paint at least one hour this week.*
3. *Eat more healthful food*	*Stop at the health food store or farmer's market and buy pleasing, healthful fruits, vegetables, and grains. Using a whole foods cookbook, create a simple, visually stimulating, and nutritious meal.*
4. *Go back to work in business again*	*Make three phone calls to explore job possibilities.*

FEMALE *(What You Want)*	MALE *(What You Can Do To Give Yourself What You Want)*
5. *Travel and adventure — see new places.*	*Get posters and travel brochures of exciting places. Hang them on the wall and begin visualizing traveling there.*

1.

2.

3.

4.

5.

FEMALE *(What You Want)*	*MALE* *(What You Can Do To* *Give Yourself What You Want)*

6.

7.

8.

9.

10.

TYRANT AND REBEL

The tyrant is that voice within us that constantly tells us what we "should" be doing. You may hear your tyrant as the voice of a domineering parent, a strict teacher, or some other authority figure that made a strong impression on you in the past. The tyrant seeks control. It is that part of each of us which is rigid and demands conformity to a narrow, strictly defined set of guidelines. In short, the tyrant is demanding, critical, and unyielding.

Our tyrant was not developed with self-abuse in mind. Its original purpose was to protect us from the external tyrant. If we could whip ourselves into shape, then we could avoid criticism and rejection by the external authority figure.

Our rebel was originally developed in response to our tyrant or other authority figures. It is that part of us that says "no" to the demands of authority figures, parents, teachers, etc. If we did not have the rebel voice that says "no" to the tyrant, we could run ourselves into the ground following the unyielding expectations of internal or external tyrants.

As the rebel developed further, however, it began to say no to anything at all resembling a "should" or demand, so that now when there is something that you really want, and you push yourself or make demands of yourself to attain it, your rebel may try to sabotage your goal directly or passively.

The rebel simply refuses to do anything others tell it to do. It can be angry, uncooperative, passive, and unyielding.

The tyrant insists on your full attention and cooperation. If you try to ignore or reject this voice (as your rebel often does), the tyrant will become frustrated and grow louder and more demanding in an attempt to be heard. The louder your tyrant becomes, the more your rebel resists. As this battle between the tyrant and rebel escalates within you, you find yourself feeling stuck. Your energy cannot move in any direction when two parts of yourself are doing battle. Even worse, as these two voices argue, their noise can actually overwhelm the sound of your true intuitive voice.

When this happens, the best response is to realize you're stuck in a no-win situation and then observe your internal conflict. As you come to understand more clearly the nature of your tyrant and rebel energies, their power over you will be diminished. Once this has happened, try to remove your energy from these voices and make contact with your inner female. Ask her for guidance. This will unblock your energy, for the true source of energy movement and power lies in listening to your intuition, receiving its guidance, and acting on it.

EXERCISE 16

In the first column, list some rules and expectations your tyrant has dictated to you. In the second column record your rebel's reactions to each demand. Some examples follow.

TYRANT	*REBEL*
1. *You have to work all the time to be successful. Work, work, work. You're lazy! Get up and **do something!***	*That's a lie. I don't have to listen to you, you slave driver. Creative geniuses need time at the beach (or the bar or wherever). I really don't feel like doing anything at all!*
2. *When are you going to stop playing the field? Grow up and get married like a responsible, respectable person.*	*Stop bothering me. You sound like my mother. I can do what I want with my body. Who needs a relationship anyway? I don't.*
3. *Stop eating all that food. You're fat. Nobody's going to want you. You'd better start dieting right away.*	*I don't care what you or anybody else thinks. I'm going to do what I want. I'll eat whatever I want.*

1.

2.

TYRANT   *REBEL*

3.

4.

5.

6.

7.

8.

TYRANT	REBEL
9.	
10.	

EXERCISE 17

Close your eyes and allow images of your tyrant and rebel to form in your mind's eye. If you don't see a clear picture, try to get a feeling or sense of what they are like. Once you have formed some impression, listen to what they have to say.

Next, in writing, describe your tyrant and rebel, giving them full color and form. You may want to give them each a name and have them talk with each other. If you like, use your colored pencils to create pictures of them, too. For example:

My tyrant is a huge woman. She wears a black miniskirt and boots. She carries a whip. She's constantly giving orders and making demands, and she expects to be obeyed. Her name is Bertha.

My rebel lies on the beach, smokes cigarettes, and eats chocolates all day long. Her name is Billie. She gazes endlessly out over the ocean and has no cares or concerns about the day.

Billie does not want to hear what Bertha says, so she ignores her. Bertha hates this, so she gets bigger, louder, and angrier. Then Billie thumbs her nose at Bertha. And so it goes, on and on.

Another example:

My tyrant is my father. He's very rational and very convincing in his explanations about the "right" way to live and how important it is to get ahead professionally and financially. He insists that I go back to college for my master's degree so I can achieve more professional success.

My rebel wears a black leather jacket and is totally uninterested in education or career. He just wants to ride a motorcycle, chase women, and do whatever feels good. He just ignores the father part.

After describing the interaction between your tyrant and your rebel, close your eyes and visualize the two of them stuck in their positions. When the image is clear, move away from them, and allow an image or feeling of your Higher Self or your intuitive wisdom to appear. Listen to what this part has to say to you. Then describe this in writing.

Example:

When I move away from my tyrant and rebel, I see an image of a wise old man in a monk's habit. He is seated on a rock in the middle of a beautiful meadow. He tells me that he has always been with me and will continue to be here when I am willing to come to him. He says the tyrant and rebel are both aspects of me, but neither one is who I really am. He can help me get in touch with a deeper sense of myself.

VICTIM AND RESCUER

Another set of polarized energies that many people carry within them are the victim and rescuer. Although each person potentially contains both energies, most people identify more with one or the other, and that's what they act out in their lives.

Victims believe they are helpless, that they have no control over what's happening to them. The victim within us does not want to accept any responsibility and so chooses to take a passive approach to life. The victim has discovered that by assuming a helpless attitude and refraining from taking direct action in any situation, the responsibility for its actions will fall elsewhere. Therefore, when something unpleasant happens to us, our victim can blame other people, events, or things for how we are feeling.

Rescuers believe that others "need" their help. Our rescuer suffers from a classic identity problem and is that part of us that believes we have no identity except in relation to others. Our rescuer feels we are really nothing unless someone needs us. In fact, our rescuer clings to these ideas in order to avoid helping itself. Thus, we spend our time trying to rescue others, instead of finding out how we ourselves feel or what we may need.

Transformation of the victim and rescuer occurs when we are willing to look within for our own healing, instead of looking outside ourselves, seeking to heal someone else (the rescuer) or be healed (the victim).

EXERCISE 18

A. Using the format below, list ways in which you see yourself as a victim now. In the first column, describe how you are a victim, and in the second list who or what you are being victimized by. Take the time to think carefully about your actions as you describe these interactions and notice how you feel.

Next, in order to empower yourself, take your focus off the situation, person, or institution that you feel victimized by and bring your thoughts back to yourself. Ask the universe to reveal to you your source of power and to heal the victim within you. Ask also what action you can take in this situation to empower yourself. Be patient. Although you may not get an immediate answer, something will come to you, perhaps right away, or within the next few hours or days. When your guidance comes, write it down in the third column. Some examples follow.

HOW YOU ARE A VICTIM	WHO OR WHAT IS VICTIMIZING YOU	ACTION YOU CAN TAKE
1. I hate my job but feel trapped: I can't quit because I need the money.	Society, money pressures, the place I work.	I can seek the services of a career counselor and explore other career possibilities.
2. My partner refuses to talk to me about his or her feelings or listen to mine. I feel shut out, alone, scared.	My partner, the uncertainty of male and female roles in our society.	I can find a supportive friend with whom I can talk things over and share my feelings. I can learn how to fulfill more of my own emotional needs. I can ask my partner to go to counseling with me.
3. I feel depressed and frightened. I don't see much meaning in life.	Life, the world.	I can reach out for help. I can call a therapist and see if talking about these feelings can help.
4. I drink a lot (or take drugs) when things get difficult. I'm not proud of my behavior but it's the only way I can cope.	Alcohol, drugs, life.	I can attend AA or other supportive recovery meetings and learn to develop my own recovery program.

1.

2.

HOW YOU ARE A VICTIM	WHO OR WHAT IS VICTIMIZING YOU	ACTION YOU CAN TAKE
3.		
4.		
5.		
6.		
7.		
8.		
9.		
10.		

B. Now, in the same way, list ways in which you are rescuing others. In the first column describe *how* you are rescuing; in the second, list *who* you are rescuing. Again, allow yourself the time to clearly examine what you are doing as you make your lists.

Next, consider each situation separately. Close your eyes and shift your focus away from the person(s) you are trying to rescue. Ask yourself if there is any part of you that feels helplessness. Ask the universe to help you answer this, to show you the needy part of yourself. Only by seeing and accepting your own needs will you be able to heal yourself and others.

Finally, ask yourself if there's anything you can do for yourself. When you receive an answer, record it in the third column. Some examples follow.

HOW I RESCUE	WHO OR WHAT I AM RESCUING	WHAT I CAN DO FOR MYSELF
1. *I'm trying to take care of other people's feelings on my job. I want everything to be calm.*	*People, chaotic situations.*	*I can start asking myself what **I** feel and what **I** need. I can learn to take care of myself so that I feel calm on the inside.*
2. *My brother keeps getting in financial messes. I keep bailing him out, because he doesn't seem to be able to manage his own life.*	*My brother.*	*I can start setting boundaries with my brother by letting him know that I won't do this any more in the future. I can take care of **my** needs and trust him to grow up and be responsible.*
3. *My husband drinks too much. I try to provide him with everything he needs so he won't have to do this but I can't seem to change his behavior.*	*My husband.*	*I need to realize that I am not responsible for my husband's life, no matter how much I love him. I need to focus on my own healing process. I can read some books on co-dependency and start attending Al-Anon meetings.*

HOW I RESCUE	WHO OR WHAT I AM RESCUING	WHAT I CAN DO FOR MYSELF
1.		
2.		
3.		
4.		
5.		
6.		

HOW I RESCUE	WHO OR WHAT I AM RESCUING	WHAT I CAN DO FOR MYSELF
7.		
8.		
9.		
10.		

EXERCISE 19

Do you identify more strongly with being a victim or a rescuer? Think back to your childhood and try to recall whether your role was that of the rescuer, the victim, or both. Were other family members playing the part of victim or rescuer? Did you learn by watching them? Did you receive feedback (in the form of attention, either negative or positive) from others that reinforced being the victim or rescuer?

In the space provided on the following page, write down any thoughts that come to mind in response to these questions. You may want to take your colored pencils and draw some of the images or feelings that you have from your childhood. Write down any other thoughts or memories that these questions stimulate.

FEELINGS

Many of us have not learned how to experience or express our feelings. Until very recently, our families and society have not placed much value on feelings or their expression. Because of this, we often overlook our own feelings. The energy of these unfelt, unexpressed feelings remains blocked in our bodies where it can cause emotional and physical discomfort and, eventually, illness and disease.

Many people are afraid to experience their so-called "negative" emotions — sadness, hurt, anger, fear, or despair. They are afraid they will be overwhelmed by these emotions if they open up to them or they may fear they will be stuck with these negative feelings forever.

Actually the opposite is true: When you are willing to fully experience a particular feeling, the blocked energy will be released and the feeling will dissolve.

The problem is, when people are uncomfortable or in pain, they don't know how to do this. We are in the habit of going about our lives simply hoping this discomfort or pain will go away.

We need to begin to give our feelings priority. We can learn how to feel our feelings and give them the expression they deserve. If we do this regularly, we need never get to the point that our pain paralyzes us with fear. The following exercises can assist you in this process.

EXERCISE 20

Close your eyes and focus your attention on the middle of your body — on your heart, your solar plexus, and your abdomen. Ask yourself how you are feeling emotionally right now. Try to distinguish the feelings from the thoughts you are having in your head. Are you feeling peaceful, excited, anxious, sad, angry, empty, joyful, frustrated, guilty, loving, lonely, fulfilled, serious, or playful?

If you find an unhappy or upset feeling inside of you, go into that feeling and give it a voice. Ask it to talk to you and tell you what it's feeling. Try to listen carefully to its point of view. Be sympathetic, loving, and supportive toward your feelings. Ask if there is anything you can do to take better care of yourself. Use the space below to record any aspects of this dialogue you may wish to remember.

For this exercise, you will need colored pens, or crayons, or even finger paints. Whichever medium you decide to use, put it in front of you on a clear table with plenty of space. Have plenty of large sheets of unlined white paper. Now take a deep breath, and notice how you feel. Are you feeling tired, anxious, happy? What color is the feeling? Pick the color from among your pens, crayons or paints that represents your feeling. Start to draw with that color, using either your dominant or nondominant hand, or both. What shape is the feeling? (Trust your impulse about this.) Use the color you've chosen and any other colors you want to draw a picture of how you are feeling — literal or abstract. Sit and look at your drawing for a while. Keep following any impulses you have to add to the drawing, using any colors and shapes that feel right to you. Don't worry about how it looks or what it means, just do what you feel. When your drawing "feels" complete, turn the paper over. Use a crayon to write three words that describe your drawing(s). Notice how you are feeling now. This exercise is not an attempt to change your feelings. It is a way of learning to accept, experience, and express your feelings. Do this exercise as often as you want.

EXERCISE 22

Moving your body, making sound, and breathing allow the body to release unexpressed emotion.

Even if you don't know how you're feeling or don't feel you have anything to release, you can do the following exercise. Be sure to notice how you feel after completing it and take the time to write down anything you may feel was significant while you did the exercise.

Stand in a comfortable position with your feet shoulder-length apart. Take several deep breaths, and as you inhale stretch your hands above your head. As you exhale, drop your hands to the floor, bending your body at the waist. Repeat this process several times, and as you inhale imagine you're scooping energy up from the earth, then straighten your body and reach to the sky. As you exhale let out a big sigh of relief, bend at the waist, and drop your hands to the floor.

Next, use your hands to pat your entire body. Lightly pat every area of your body. This touching will energize you — it lets your body know that you know it's there.

When you feel energized, move your body around. Twist your body from side to side and shake out your arms and hands. Pick your feet up and put them down, and as you do this, make sounds — any expression of sound will be helpful, even weird sounds. Then shake everything out — your feet, legs, hands, and head. Continue to make sounds as you do this.

After moving around for five to ten minutes, mound several pillows into a pile and pound them with your fists or a plastic baseball bat. Be sure to express sound as you do this. Scream and make noise for all the times you didn't and wished you had. If you want, you can scream into the pillows.

Allow yourself five or ten minutes or more to do this, and then, when you feel finished, let yourself rest. Find a comfortable place to sit or lie down. As you rest notice how your body feels, and how you feel emotionally.

DAILY LIFE

In this section we will learn how to live the principles we've been learning by applying them to the practical, everyday concerns of life: money, work, play, health, body image, relationships, sexuality, and children. As you follow your inner guidance and apply it to these concerns, you will move toward aliveness, health, prosperity, and creativity.

MONEY

The creative energy of the universe is limitless and readily available to us at all times. Money is a symbol of our creative energy so, potentially, money is also readily available to us. The extent to which we are willing and able to express our creative energy effectively in the world determines how much money will be in our lives. A lack of money reflects the energy blockages within ourselves.

If you are not doing what you really love to do, if you don't believe you deserve to receive, if your intuition nudges you to take action and you ignore it, then your energy will be blocked; consequently, your money flow will be blocked as well. If you are doing what you love to do, and are willing to receive a return from your actions, the universe will reward you with an abundant flow of money in your life. As you learn to trust yourself and follow your inner guidance, you align yourself with the higher creative power which can provide for you on all levels, including the financial. To achieve financial balance and harmony in your life, you need to develop and integrate both the masculine principle of "doing" and expressing energy and the feminine principle of "being" and receiving energy.

Remember that true prosperity coming from an alignment of spirit and form does not involve excessive amounts of money to squander or waste. It involves an appropriate flow of money to do what you truly want in life and live a lifestyle that is in harmony with your being and with the earth.

EXERCISE 23

This meditation may help to free you of blocks to abundance you may have and give you a vision of what prosperity is for you.

MEDITATION — MONEY

Start by breathing deeply for a few moments. Imagine that you're drawing a golden light into your body through your feet. As you inhale, the light moves upward through your entire body, and as you exhale, it streams from the top of your head like a fountain, surrounding you with golden light.

Slowly inhale and feel this light filling all the cells of your body with abundance, limitless opportunity, joy, creativity, and inner knowing. As you exhale, the light surrounds you with energy and power. Continue to draw the light in through you and surround yourself with it. As you do so, feel it dissolve any old ideas, negative beliefs, or blockages you have in your life. Visualize this light moving through you and healing you, transforming you into an open channel for prosperity. Spend a few moments with this image.

Next, imagine that this energy is now mirrored in your world. You now have total abundance in your life. Take stock of your new status. What is your living environment like? What is your home like? What are you doing as a career? How are you expressing your creativity? What are your ideal relationships like? Thoroughly visualize how this prosperity has affected every aspect of your life.

If any negative thoughts surface, let them float by for now and stay gently focused on the prosperity that is yours, the wealth that is being mirrored in your life by the energy moving through your body. Visualize your prosperity exactly the way you would like it to be.

When you're ready, release this image, bring your awareness back into yourself, and feel yourself return to the room. Write a description of what you saw during this meditation and include a description of your ideal and prosperous life. You may want to pretend that you're writing about this to a friend. For example: Dear Susan, You should see my life. I am feeling great about myself and what has happened for me. My photography career has taken off. I am now doing portrait photography on a full-time basis. I am making enough money to do many of the things I've always wanted to do. I am taking a trip to Africa next spring . . . etc.

We can go within to seek answers to all we need to know. In this exercise you will ask your inner guidance to show you what is blocking your energy and, therefore, financial prosperity in your life.

Close your eyes and breathe deeply. Relax into a deep, quiet place inside, and ask to be in touch with your inner guidance. Ask yourself, "How am I blocking the flow of energy and wealth into my life now?" Be open to receive whatever answer might come to you, in words or an image. The answer may come right away or it may come in the next few hours, days, or weeks, so don't be discouraged if you don't receive an answer right away.

The answer you seek can take any form. Your intuition might show you the face of someone with whom you have unfinished business, or perhaps your inner voice will give you a direct suggestion, such as, "Learn to say no more often" or "Take more risks." The guidance you receive may be something totally unexpected and may even seem unrelated to work or money. Whatever happens, trust what you hear, simply allow it to come forth.

When you have completed this first part of the exercise, make a list of the results. In the first column, list the ways that, according to your intuition, you are blocking yourself. In the second column, include any action you can take to unblock that energy so greater wealth can come to you now. Some examples follow.

HOW I AM BLOCKING MYSELF	*WHAT I CAN DO ABOUT IT*
1. *I've been pushing myself because I'm afraid if I stop, no money will come in.*	*Take a day or two off from work and do things that are nourishing to myself, to open my ability to receive.*
2. *I hold onto money tightly because I'm afraid I won't have enough.*	*Decide to give a small amount to a cause I support and see how I feel and what happens. Go out and buy something I want for myself now.*
3. *I'm still angry at my ex-wife about our financial settlement.*	*Write all my angry, hurt feelings in a letter and read it to a friend that I trust. Then burn the letter and ask my Higher Power to release me from carrying this resentment.*

HOW I AM BLOCKING MYSELF	WHAT I CAN DO ABOUT IT
1.	
2.	
3.	
4.	
5.	

EXERCISE 25

Draw a picture (or make a collage using pictures and words cut from magazines) of yourself living an abundant life on all levels — physical (material), emotional, mental, and spiritual. Include pictures or symbols of everything that's important to you on all these levels.

WORK AND PLAY

Work can feel as good as play. When you follow your energy and do what you truly want, the distinction between work and play begins to dissolve. Work will no longer be what you have to do and play what you want to do. When you are doing what you love, you may work harder and produce more than ever before, but it will often feel like play.

Finding our right work is an evolving process. At times it may be appropriate to do work that we don't love in order to learn certain skills, or just to pay the bills while we are exploring, discovering, and growing in other ways. Also, our needs and desires change as we grow, so work that was suitable and enjoyable at one stage may be unfulfilling at another time.

So if you find yourself in a less than fully satisfying job, don't put yourself down or think you are doing something wrong. Just recognize that you are probably beginning to outgrow it, and start thinking, fantasizing, and investigating other possibilities.

The way to discover your right work at any stage of your life is to observe what you most love to do or feel interested in doing and then take steps to do it. Your fantasies can tell you how you really want to be expressing yourself. Remember, the job you are seeking may not exist yet — it may be up to you to create it. The exercises that follow may help you discover your true work and dissolve the distinctions between work and play in your life.

EXERCISE 26

Exploring your fantasies is a good first step toward finding work you love. Even very unrealistic fantasies, although they may not ever manifest in form, will help move you in the right direction for exploration and discovery.

In the first column, list the fantasies and dreams you entertain around work, career, and creativity. Then, visualize yourself doing what you've written down. For example, see yourself tap dancing on Broadway. Feel what it would be like for you to do what you love to do. Out of visualization often comes an inspiration for action.

In the second column, describe any actions you can take to explore your fantasies. Don't try to do all of these things at once or you will get overwhelmed. Choose one or two and try them. In a month or two check the list again and see if you want to try another option. Let the next six months or a year be a time of exploring and discovering the work that you would love to do. Examples follow.

FANTASIES AND IMPULSES	*ACTION*
1. Tap Dance on Broadway	*Call local dance studios and explore adult tap classes. Later, seek out a community theater group that may put together shows. Suggest a "dance show" and enlist to tap!*
2. Open my own ski shop.	*Talk to the owner of the ski shop I go to and find out more about the business.*
1.	
2.	
3.	
4.	

FANTASIES AND IMPULSES	ACTION
5.	
6.	
7.	
8.	
9.	
10.	

EXERCISE 27

Write down ten things you love to do, even if they don't seem to be work-related.

Examples:

1. *Organize things*	2. *Watch soap operas*
3. *Talk with people*	4. *Travel*
5. *Swim*	6. *Cook*
7. *Rearrange the furniture*	8. *Buy clothes for myself and others*
9. *Lift weights*	10. *Balance my checkbook*

1.   2.

3.   4.

5.   6.

7.   8.

9.   10.

Now, close your eyes and imagine yourself doing some of these things and getting paid well for it. Take 5–10 minutes every day and repeat the visualization. If negative thoughts come up — for instance if you find yourself saying that you couldn't possibly be paid for watching television — gently refocus your thoughts back to the positive. We sometimes close ourselves off to new opportunities by not believing they are possible. Suppose, for instance, that you have written cooking and traveling on your list, and a week after you've been doing your visualization you get an urge to call an old friend. You phone him — and he just happens to mention a job he's heard about for a cook on a cruise ship!

EXERCISE 28

Affirmations can help you to create what you want for yourself. Pick two of the affirmations below or make up some of your own and write them 10–20 times per day. Say them in front of a mirror in a firm voice. This can be very powerful.

1. I, *(your name)*, am now doing what I love to do and am richly rewarded for it.
2. I, _____, am now an open channel for creative ideas.
3. I, _____, now know exactly what I want to do to make plenty of money.
4. My work feels like play.
5. I, _____, trust the energy within me and am guided to my perfect job.

Use the space below to create your own affirmations.

1.

2.

3.

4.

5.

HEALTH

The body is the barometer of our emotions. We may be able in our minds to deny what we are feeling, but our body always knows. If we let it, it can show us what is or is not working in our thinking, self-expression, and lifestyle. It can also tell us whether or not we have been trusting or ignoring our intuitive voice. When we *do* trust ourselves, our bodies reflect this in increased health, aliveness, and beauty. When we don't trust ourselves and fail to follow our inner guidance, our aliveness decreases and our body reflects this in a loss of vitality, numbness, pain, and, eventually, physical disease.

Disease is a message sent by our bodies to tell us that we are not following our true energy or supporting our feelings. The body will continue to send signals until we get the message. These signals will start with relatively subtle feelings of tiredness and discomfort, and increase in urgency and intensity if we fail to pay attention and make the appropriate changes. We will receive increasingly stronger signals, including aches, pains, and minor illnesses, and if we still don't change, a serious or fatal illness or accident may eventually occur.

If you are suffering from physical discomfort or disease, rest. When you are quiet, ask your body what message your illness is conveying to you. Your body will always attempt to tell you what you need in order to heal yourself. The following exercises can help you learn to communicate more clearly with your body and may help you uncover the cause of any disease you may be experiencing.

Obviously these exercises should be done in conjunction with appropriate medical attention, or other healing modalities, for specific problems.

EXERCISE 29

MEDITATION

If a particular part of your body is sick or in pain, this meditation may help. Make yourself comfortable, take a few deep breaths, and completely relax your body and mind. Now direct your consciousness to the part of your body that needs healing and ask that part what it is feeling and what it is trying to tell you. Be receptive to feeling and hearing what your body's message is. Ask that part of your body what you need to do to heal yourself. Pay attention to and follow whatever it tells you.

If you have difficulty doing this process in meditation, try this written exercise. Get two colored pens. With your dominant hand, write a question to your body. With your other hand, and using the other colored pen, write spontaneously whatever comes to mind in answer to the question. At first it may be difficult to write with your nondominant hand, but do the best you can. Your dominant hand speaks for your conscious mind which is desiring information. Your nondominant hand speaks for your unconscious or intuitive mind, in this case representing the body's feelings.

For example:

Greg's dominant hand: Back, why are you aching?

Greg's nondominant hand (speaking for the back): I'm carrying too much weight. I have too much responsibility. I need support.

Greg's dominant hand: What kind of support?

Greg's nondominant hand: I need Greg to have someone he can talk to about his feelings and problems. He tries to handle everything himself. Then I feel like I'm carrying the weight of the world on my shoulders.

MEDITATION

A. Poor health often can be the result of unexpressed emotion. Many people who suffer from serious diseases have a history of suppressing their feelings. If you are experiencing any disease in your life, this meditation may help you begin to uncover and express any feelings that may be causing your illness.

Close your eyes and take a few deep breaths. As you relax, feel yourself let go of external concerns and gradually drop within yourself to your intuition. From this deep place within, allow an image of someone to come forward. This may be someone with whom you need to express some feelings, someone you've wanted to say something to for a long time, or someone with whom you have recently felt uncomfortable. It can be a "positive" or "negative" communication.

When this person is clearly before you, imagine you are saying whatever you have wanted to communicate to that person. Let out any and all unexpressed thoughts or feelings. Remember, any feelings you hold in are only hurting you. Unexpressed anger, which leads to resentment, is a major cause of disease in the body.

After you have expressed everything you need to say, tell this person, "I now release you (or I am now willing to release you) to your highest good," or, "I am willing to release you to the universe." Take a few deep breaths, and know that you have expressed and released everything you need to for right now.

Often, this process can make us aware of many things we have suppressed, so you may think you've said everything you need to say and then a few hours later or a few days later more feelings will surface and need to be expressed. If so, redo the above exercise as often as you want or do Part B.

B. You can also communicate any unexpressed feelings with a person by writing them a letter. On the next page or on a separate piece of paper, write a letter to someone with whom you have needed to communicate. Write everything you can think of that you've wanted to say. This is a time to express any thoughts you've had about the past, present, or future and a time to express all your feelings of blame, anger, hurt, sadness, love, etc. This is a safe place to express any feelings that have been buried within you and which may have been causing disease to your body. As you write you may get in touch with different emotions. For example, you may begin writing about anger and then begin expressing sadness, fear, and love. Trust your feelings and let them flow.

When you are finished, tear out this sheet and burn the letter. This will symbolize that you are emotionally letting go.

Again, if you find yourself feeling more feelings or having other thoughts that need to be expressed, redo this exercise or Part A.

It may or may not be necessary to communicate any of these feelings to the person in question. Once you have done the meditation or written processes one or more times, you may discover that you are gaining greater clarity about your feelings or are getting down to the essence of what's really bothering you. Just acknowledging these feelings to yourself may well be enough to heal them, especially if the person is no longer physically present in your life. However, if you feel the need to communicate with the person, write a real letter saying what you need to say as clearly and simply as possible and then send it. Remember that if you can state the essence of your hurt or anger in a clear, direct way with as little blame or judgment as possible, you will have a better chance of being heard. Be sure to ask for what you want. Do this for your own clearing and healing, letting go of any particular expected response. If you have succeeded in expressing your deepest feelings, you will feel relieved and released. You may need to do this with more than one person — including parents, spouses, ex-lovers, friends, children. Following is an example of such a letter.

> *Susan,*
>
> *I need to write this letter to express my feelings to you so that I don't carry them around inside of me anymore. I'm very hurt and angry that you have chosen to end our friendship without sharing with me your feelings or your reasons for doing so. I believe our friendship deserves better treatment than this. I'm hurt that you didn't trust me enough to tell me honestly what was going on for you. I have a lot of resentment about the way you handled this, which I'm trying to clear and release by writing to you, since it's very uncomfortable for me to have these kinds of feelings. I'd like you to write to me and tell me your feelings. It might help to clear things up.*
>
> *Jane*

To be truly full of health, we also need to learn to use our bodies physically in a way that is fun and joyful. Exercise too often implies *work*. We need to make our physical exercise more like play. Think of very young children, or animals. They don't need to go to the gym and work out to stay in shape. They move their bodies instinctively, stretching and running in ways that are simple and playful. This exercise will help you to put joy in your movements.

Find an area in your home with a good deal of open space. Move furniture around if you need to — just enough so that you have a clear area for about one body length in either direction. Put on some music that represents your mood currently, or a mood you would like to be in right now. Are you feeling excited, tired, somewhat edgy, or overextended? Stand in the middle of the space you have just created and start to move your head to the music. Without any strain or effort, slowly let your head move and change, remembering to let your jaw hang loose. As the music plays, let your body start to move with it, slowly letting each part of the body join in, similar to the tuning up of an orchestra. Let the shoulders join in when they're ready, let the hands find their expression. Slowly let yourself work your way down your body until all the parts of you are "playing in the orchestra." When you've reached your feet, start to move back up the body and include all the parts of your body that want to move, always remembering the rhythm of the music. Continue playing music and moving to it as long as it feels good. When you feel finished, sit or lie down for a few minutes and reflect on how your body feels. Where do you feel some loosening of your muscles? Where do you feel you need to stretch? Complete this exercise by noting these body parts and either stretch them right now or remember them for tomorrow or the next time you repeat this exercise. Notice how you feel emotionally. This is an excellent time to spend a few minutes meditating, saying affirmations, or just relaxing.

EXERCISE 32

In the space below, describe what perfect health for you would be like. How would you look, feel, and act? Include spiritual, mental, emotional as well as physical aspects of health. Now, visualize what you describe, and affirm that this state of perfect health is a reality in your life right now.

YOUR PERFECT BODY

Your perfect body is the one you already have. It's the body your spirit has created as your expression in physical form. To get a sense of how beautiful our bodies really are, watch a group of young children playing naturally together. Though they may be quite different in size, coloring, and shape, they are each beautiful in their own way. Watch animals in a natural setting and see how beautiful they are. Young children and animals are so beautiful because they are filled with life force and move freely with that energy. Unfortunately, as we grow up we are conditioned not to trust and follow our life energy. Our bodies pay the price. Also, most civilized human beings have not learned to love, appreciate, or care for our bodies, and our bodies begin to show this lack of love and care. To allow your body to express its true beauty, you must develop a loving, supportive relationship with it. This can take time and patience.

The health and well-being of our bodies is strongly connected to our emotional well-being. We are much more likely to be physically healthy, vital, and attractive if and when we are feeling emotionally secure and fulfilled. Our emotional wounds, conflicts, and blocks are often expressed physically in our bodies. Our feelings about our bodies are connected to our core feelings about our identity and self-worth. Therefore, our body issues are deep and complex. There are no simple solutions, but if we are willing to do the inner work of emotional and spiritual healing as well as physical healing, our problems with our bodies can lead us to wholeness on all levels.

One of the most common ways that our emotional difficulties manifest physically is in our relationship to food, through weight problems (overweight or underweight) and eating disorders. Our relationship with food has deep emotional roots, connected with our childhood feelings toward our families, and with issues of scarcity, nurturing, self-love, personal boundaries, and intimacy.

We are an addictive society and a great many people these days have an addictive relationship to food. That is, we use food compulsively to control or suppress emotions, to fill emotional needs, to avoid confronting other issues, and so on.

If you have food addictions, the exercises in this chapter, while possibly providing some valuable insight, will not be sufficient to help you deal with the problem. They may not even be appropriate for you, at least until you do the primary work of confronting and healing the addictive behavior with professional or group support.

If you do have addictive patterns with food or any eating disorder such as serious overeating, anorexia, or bulimia, I urge you to seek professional counseling. There are many wonderful therapists and programs specializing in these problems. And there is Overeaters Anonymous, a twelve-step program with free meetings in most cities.

If you do not have food addictions or serious body issues, or you have already done effective work on them, you may find that the exercises in this chapter can help you restore a natural, trusting relationship with your body.

Having a beautiful body starts with following the natural flow of your energy. This means trying to sleep, eat, rest, and move when *you* want. It means learning to trust yourself.

The main obstacle to trusting ourselves is that most of us have not yet learned how. As children, we unquestioningly adopt parental and societal rules, habits, and thoughts about how we treat our bodies. These include eating at times convenient to others, not ourselves, and finishing our plates in order to receive a reward. Even as adults, although we may have radically changed our childhood habits, our lifestyles are still based on our reactions to external pressures and attitudes. Grown up though we may be, we have yet to establish a direct connection to our true, spontaneous nature — our essential self. Because of this, it is difficult to understand and respond to the natural needs of our bodies.

In learning to trust yourself, you must first risk acting on what your body is telling you. In the beginning you may receive information only from your head, rather than your intuition, but the more you risk acting on what you hear inside yourself, the more you will open your inner channel and the clearer your intuitive messages will become.

Your body knows what's good for it, and you need to be open to whatever it might request of you, whether it is to stay in bed or to get up early and work hard the whole day long. At first you may find yourself doing the opposite of everything you have been doing. For example, if you've been working constantly you may want to spend a few days (or months!) resting, relaxing, and playing, doing what you've been denying yourself. Or, if you tend toward lethargy, you may need to get your body moving. Let yourself experiment as much as possible. Eventually you will find a balance, and this time it will stem from that deep source of balance within.

The following exercises can help identify negative beliefs or old attitudes you've had about your body and pave the way for a more deeply intuitive understanding of what you truly need.

EXERCISE 33

Sit down and reflect on all the old ideas and beliefs you have about your body, food, and exercise. Try to go back and recall everything anyone ever told you about food. These may be statements you heard from your mother or father, or beliefs acquired from television or magazines. Let them all come to the surface. Write down as many as you can think of. Next to each one, write an affirmation that will balance these beliefs. Examples follow.

NEGATIVE BELIEFS	AFFIRMATIONS
1. *I don't like my body.*	*I love and appreciate my body.*
2. *I'm too fat (or too thin).*	*My body is beautiful.*
3. *I gain weight every time I look at food.*	*I can safely enjoy looking at and eating food because my body is slender and healthy.*
4. *I eat all the wrong foods.*	*I desire and enjoy natural, healthy, nutritious food.*
5. *I'll never have the kind of body I want.*	*I, (your name), now have the body I want.*
6. *It's hard for me to exercise.*	*I now exercise easily and effortlessly. I enjoy exercising. I express my body freely through a form of exercise I love.*

1.

	NEGATIVE BELIEFS	*AFFIRMATIONS*
2.		
3.		
4.		
5.		
6.		
7.		
8.		
9.		
10.		

Using any old ideas and beliefs you have had about your body, describe how you have been controlling yourself rather than following your natural rhythm. Next to each statement list ways you are willing to let go of this control and allow your natural rhythm to come through.

If you are accustomed to controlling yourself, letting go can be an uncomfortable experience. Initially you may want to practice doing this in one area of your life only. Move on to the next area only when you are comfortable with this process. Some examples follow.

HOW I CONTROL	*WAYS TO LET GO*
1. *I push myself to keep going when I'm really tired.*	*For one week, I can rest when my body wants to rest, instead of pushing myself.*
2. *I am constantly on a "controlled" diet where I deprive myself of almost everything I really like.*	*For one week, instead of dieting, I'll let myself eat what I really want.*
3. *I insist that I run five miles a day whether I feel like it or not.*	*This week, I will let myself run only when I want and, then, only as far as I want.*

1.

2.

3.

4.

HOW I CONTROL	*WAYS TO LET GO*
5.	
6.	
7.	
8.	
9.	
10.	

EXERCISE 35

Learning to appreciate and love yourself is an important part of developing your perfect body. All things grow more beautiful when they are nourished by love and appreciation.

In the space below, write down as many things as you can think of that you can do to appreciate yourself. Be sure to focus on things you can do for your body.

Examples:

1. *Take a hot bath.*
2. *Buy fresh flowers for myself.*

3. Eat a delicious gourmet meal of natural, healthful foods.
4. Splurge on a professional massage.
5. Go swimming.
6. Plan a weekend away.
7. Take a half a day just to pamper myself — eat a wonderful meal, listen to classical music, and lie around relaxing.
8. Take a long, solitary walk and enjoy the pleasure of my own company.
9. Join a health club and go twice a week.
10. Put on my favorite music and dance.
11. Make love.

1.

2.

3.

4.

5.

6.

7.

8.

9.

10.

If you always wait (weight) to be, do, or have what you want, your energy will become blocked and your body will reflect this in excess weight. By expressing yourself directly and doing *what* you want, *when* you want, energy will move freely through your body, and this energy circulation will dissolve your excess weight.

What have you been "weighting" for — what have you been "weighting" to say, do, or be? In one column write down anything you have been "weighting" to do.

Is there anything you'd like to change about this? In the second column, list what you would like to do to put a stop to your "weighting." If you do want to take action on some of the issues you've been "weighting" to handle, you may want to put a date by your plans to solidify your action. Examples follow.

WHAT I AM "WEIGHTING" FOR	ACTION I WILL TAKE
1. *I've been wanting to do more dancing and always say I'll have more time later, but I never make room for it.*	*I'm going to take one dance class a week starting this week.*
2. *I keep wanting to call my ex-husband and confront him with the fact that he still owes me $10,000.*	*Take an assertiveness class, then call or write him.*

WHAT I AM "WEIGHTING" FOR	ACTION I WILL TAKE
3. I want to straighten things out with my brother. I'd like to risk sharing my feelings with him.	I'll start by writing out what I want to say to him and then call him on (date).
4. I keep "weighting" for the right time to ask my boss for a raise.	First I'll talk over with a friend my fears about doing this. Then I'll ask my boss for a raise by the end of the month.
5. I keep "weighting" to look beautiful until I have lost weight.	I can buy a dress that makes me look beautiful right now at my current weight. I can make an effort to look pretty now.
6. I want to tell my brother-in-law that he can't stay with us anymore, but I'm afraid to.	I'll just have to take the risk to be honest with him.

1.

2.

3.

WHAT I AM "WEIGHTING" FOR	*ACTION I WILL TAKE*
4.	
5.	
6.	
7.	

8.

9.

10.

EXERCISE 37

Many people use food to change their natural energy level. Those with too much nervous energy may use it to slow themselves down, and people who feel a need for a pick-up may eat sugar or drink coffee or other stimulants to try to "get going." This use of food, however, interferes with and distorts the body's natural rhythm and flow of energy.

What would happen if you were not controlling your energy with food? If you didn't have to stop yourself from being who you are, what would your energy be like?

Take a moment to relax, then close your eyes and drop into that deepest place inside yourself. Ask your intuition to reveal an image of your true energy — of what you would be like if you were not using anything to pace or change yourself.

Describe this in the space below.

RELATIONSHIPS

When we think about relationships we think of an external process — our fulfillment will come from outside ourselves, from another person. The first step we take to create a satisfying relationship is to look for someone else to satisfy our needs. But the key to successful relationships is actually *within* us, so it is no wonder that in looking outside ourselves for fulfillment we often experience disappointment, resentment, and frustration.

Truly satisfying relationships begin inside us. Our one true relationship is our relationship with ourself. All other relationships are simply mirrors of it. Therefore, if we believe we are unlovable or if we are constantly critical of ourselves, we will continue to attract people and create situations that reinforce this belief. Conversely, as we learn to love ourselves we will automatically receive the love and appreciation from others that we desire. If we are committed to ourselves and to the truth, we will attract others with equal commitment.

The following exercise may help you see how your beliefs about relationships directly affect the relationships you have, and it will give you an opportunity to create new beliefs that can fulfill you on the inside as well as the outside.

EXERCISE 38

Think back to all the primary relationships you've had. In the space below, give a brief description of each of them. What were they like? How did you feel about them? What happened? Do you see any patterns repeating themselves? Examples follow.

My Relationships

1. *I went out with John, who seemed very interested in me but as soon as I became more interested in him, he seemed to withdraw. We broke up when I discovered he was seeing another woman.*

2. *I dated Steve, who pursued me for a long time until I agreed to go out. But he became more and more involved in his work and hardly had any time to see me. We broke up when he got a job out of state.*

1.

2.

3.

4.

5.

Once you identify a pattern or patterns, ask yourself how this reflects your internal relationship with yourself. For example, if I am attracted to critical people, this means I am being critical of myself, or if I am attracted to people who are emotionally supportive of me, this means I am supportive of myself. If people abandon me, it's an indication that I emotionally abandon myself. Sometimes the answers may not seem so evident. If so, ask the universe to reveal to you your part in the pattern and be open to gaining more insight about your process. Caution: Often we are not aware of how much we control our relationships until we look at these patterns. Once you see what you've been doing, your tendency will be to blame yourself. Don't. The point here is to see that you have the power to change the pattern of your relationships by working on your relationship with yourself, not to get hung up wishing you'd behaved differently in the past. You can always ask the universe for help in healing this pattern.

Write down your patterns and your solutions to them in the space below.

MY PATTERNS	*FINDINGS AND SOLUTIONS*
1. *I find myself continually attracted to emotionally needy men (or women) like my father (or my mother).*	*My partners mirror a needy part of myself, a part that didn't get enough love and care when I was a child. I need to get in touch with that child in me and learn to take care of it.*
2. *When I've been in a relationship for three to six months, I always want out. I want to start dating other people. I think there's something wrong with me.*	*I have a hard time standing up for myself and being honest in a relationship. I give up my individuality to the relationship and then I feel smothered and controlled. I can accept the way I am, instead of criticizing myself for this. I can begin to explore, through counseling, how I can assert myself in relationships so I won't have to run away from them.*

MY PATTERNS   *FINDINGS AND SOLUTIONS*

1.

2.

3.

4.

5.

EXERCISE 39

Our past is often our most valuable teacher. In reviewing your life, are there times you wish you had followed your energy or trusted your instincts with someone or some situation, and you didn't? Write down these experiences.

Examples:

1. *I felt pressured to go out with Stan because he was someone my mother approved of. I wish I hadn't wasted my time.*
2. *I always wish I'd gone out with that guy in my theatre class in college, but I didn't because I felt too insecure.*
3. *I never talk to girls I really want to go out with. I know they won't like me.*

1.

2.

3.

4.

5.

Now take each of these memories, close your eyes, and visualize an image of yourself standing before you. Talk to yourself (out loud or internally). Tell yourself how you feel about each memory. If you blame yourself, express it. If you feel sad or frightened, express that. When you are done, tell the image of yourself what you learned from not doing what you might have.

Next allow yourself to let go of each memory. You may want to say to yourself, "I understand and let go," or "I am now willing to release you," or "I am now willing to forgive you for this."

Is there anyone or any persons in your life *now* that you are attracted to in any way, but with whom you have been afraid to follow your energy? Write about this in the space below.

EXERCISE 40

What would it be like to have a passionate love affair with yourself? What would it be like to follow your inner guidance — your energy — from moment to moment, to create and express beauty within and without? What would it be like to feel passionate about yourself and give yourself all the attention and care an impassioned lover would give you? Use the space below to describe it. Describe the richest, most alive life possible.

EXERCISE 41

Write a description of your ideal relationship. Include important things like how you feel about each other, how you communicate, how you treat each other, what you enjoy doing together, and so on. Make it as real as possible.

Now ask yourself what part of you is afraid of having this, or is preventing you from creating this? Why? What is that part of you afraid ot? Write your honest answers to these questions, as best you can. This is a process that will help you become aware of your own inner conflicts about relationships, and begin to clear them.

Note: Relationships are a complex, challenging, and fascinating area of our lives, from which we can learn a great deal. One of the best books to help us understand and learn from our relationships is *Embracing Each Other* by Dr. Hal Stone and Dr. Sidra Winkelman, New World Library, 1989.

SEXUALITY AND PASSION

Our level of sexual energy and passion directly reflects our willingness to trust the universe within us. Sexual energy is the life force, the creative force of the universe. The more we trust ourselves and respond spontaneously to this energy, the more freely and fully the life force will move through us. When we're not afraid to experience and express all of our feelings, we come alive. We feel everything more deeply, and everything we do has an ecstatic, orgasmic quality. And when we express our deepest feelings, sexuality takes its natural place in our lives.

Unfortunately, most of us are quite skillful at cutting off our sexual energy. We instinctively know that our sexual energy has the power to create and transform our lives. There is nothing safe, stable, or sedentary about it. Not knowing how to trust the universe within, we become afraid of ourselves and afraid of where our sexual energy will take us. The universe is pure energy waiting to pour through us, but the idea of such unlimited power is frightening to us, so we respond by trying to package or control the energy. We set up rules and guidelines designed to strictly control its flow. Instead of trusting ourselves from moment to moment, we try to keep our sexuality separate from our other feelings and emotions.

Each person's sexual energy is unique. We each have our particular sexual rhythm and expression. Once we free ourselves of all our rules and limitations we'll be able to discover our natural flow. We will continually find new ways to express ourselves sexually as we find it is possible to let go of the old and allow a new way to come through.

The following exercises may help bring some of your previously suppressed thoughts and feelings about sex to the surface and help you to see how your beliefs are reflected in your sexual relationships. These exercises can also increase your awareness of your sexual energy and the energy around you.

EXERCISE 42

When we were growing up, we encountered many different and contradictory beliefs about sex. Perhaps our innocent expressions of sexuality were cut off, or perhaps a religious organization implied that sexuality was somehow evil. Contradicting this were a barrage of sexual images from television, magazines, and movies that implied that sex was what we should be seeking. Think back to the ideas and beliefs about sex you acquired while growing up and those you have now. List them in the space below.

When you have finished, take all of these old beliefs and ideas that have been running your life and turn them into affirmations. Some examples follow.

NEGATIVE BELIEFS	AFFIRMATIONS
1. I can't trust myself when it comes to my sexual desires.	I now trust myself completely. I trust and express my feelings, including my sexual feelings.
2. I can't have sex with anyone unless my body looks better.	I love and accept my body. I now have a sexual partner who loves and appreciates me and my body.
3. I want too much or too little sex.	I now trust my sexual rhythm. I tune into what I want and allow myself to have it.

1.

2.

NEGATIVE BELIEFS   AFFIRMATIONS

5.

6.

7.

8.

	NEGATIVE BELIEFS	AFFIRMATIONS
9.		
10.		

EXERCISE 43

The following meditation will take you back to an embarrassing or painful memory and assist you in healing the wound it has left. You may want to do this exercise with a close friend or therapist who can support you in expressing your feelings. If you're doing this with a friend, you may want to take turns leading each other in the meditation.

One word of caution. Many people have experienced frightening or painful sexual experiences in childhood or youth. Sometimes these painful memories have been repressed or buried. If any frightening or overwhelming memories surface during this meditation, it's *very* important to seek professional counseling or therapy to support you in uncovering and healing the wound.

MEDITATION

Close your eyes, take a deep breath, and slowly relax your entire body. Take another deep breath and relax your mind. Continue taking deep breaths, relaxing as deeply as possible.

With each breath, let yourself drop into a core place inside, a quiet place of strength and wisdom and power and inner knowing.

Next, imagine yourself walking down a beautiful path in nature. Feel the earth under your feet, experience the sun on your body and the wildlife around you.

Walk farther and farther down the path until you come to a beautiful meadow. Explore the beauty of the meadow and create a safe place for yourself to be. Find a comfortable place to sit or lie down. When you are comfortable, allow yourself to go back to a particularly embarrassing or painful sexual memory from your past. Take the first thing that arises and let yourself observe this memory. You'll only see as much as you're willing to see. Keep breathing. Bring all the events surrounding the memory into clearer focus. Who's there? Were you by yourself? Are other people there? Is one other person there? Take note of any particular smells or sounds, or any visual images that you see. Notice how you're feeling.

When you have thoroughly explored your memory, remove yourself from it and take a moment simply to relax. When you are ready, you can return to it, and then you can use creative visualization to re-create this event for yourself. You can visualize yourself taking back your power. After all, when you first experienced this incident, you were unable to do that. This is why the event was painful. This time you can say something or do something that will put you back in control so that you can determine the outcome you truly want.

What would you have done differently during this incident? Is there something you wish you had said? Or do you wish you had had someone there to protect you or take care of you? Do you need to express anger, rage, or hurt? Whatever you need, this is your opportunity to make sure you get it. Perhaps you'll want to surround yourself and the incident with golden light. Perhaps you want to change the entire thing. Perhaps you just want to say one thing or make one sound for yourself there. Whatever you want, feel yourself going back and doing it now.

When you feel ready, just release your memory and visualize yourself once again in the core place inside you — the place of your intuition, of peace and wisdom, your inner sanctuary. Take some deep breaths and gradually return to the room that you are in. When you're ready, open your eyes and come back to the here and now. If you want to, write about or draw what you experienced.

EXERCISE 44

Everything is made up of energy. The life force that flows through everyone and everything is very sensual. Young children experience everything sensuously and can express their sensuousness safely and innocently. Now you can give yourself the opportunity to do the same. Go through a day and experience and see everything you encounter as a sensual experience. For example, when you wake up in the morning feel the pleasurable sensation of lying in bed, stretching and yawning. Dress yourself in clothes that feel good to your body. Stretch and move in ways that feel good. Eat foods that look wonderful and taste delicious. Listen to music you love. Notice how things smell. Spend time outdoors, feeling everything. Give and/or receive a massage. Sit close to someone or cuddle an animal. Just have fun with the natural, beautiful, sensuous life energy that flows through you and through everything around you.

For those of you who have a partner, you can extend this exercise. Take a day or even a few hours and enjoy them sensuously with your partner as above, *without* moving into a specifically sexual interaction. Allow yourselves to feel each other's bodies — through cuddling, touching, or relaxing massage. *Do not* let these actions lead to a sexual experience. The goal is to allow yourselves the freedom to explore and enjoy without the pressure of bringing these experiences to sexual consummation.

OUR CHILDREN

Deeply intimate relationships serve as our strongest mirrors — intimate partners will often express the feelings we have suppressed in ourselves. Children, in particular, can be mirrors of our feelings. Due to their uninhibited nature, they will often express or "act out" the feelings we have bottled up inside.

For example, if you try to appear calm and collected when inside you feel upset and angry, your children may reflect these feelings by becoming wild and disruptive. No matter how hard you may try to maintain control, they will tune into the chaotic energy inside you and reflect it in their behavior. Children are very sensitive to our true feelings. If you are not expressing your feelings they will often do this for you.

Of course, most parents seek to protect their children from the problems and frustrations they themselves must face each day. They feel that sharing such feelings will only disturb children who may be too young to fully understand "adult" problems. But effective sharing does not mean dumping your anger on your children or involving them in the details of your concerns. You simply need to let your children know how you are truly feeling. For example, you might say, "I'm feeling really upset and frustrated because I've had a hard day. I'm mad at the world and at myself and at you. It's not your fault that I'm feeling this way. It would help, though, if you would go outside for a few minutes so I can have some peace and quiet to try to sort out my feelings." If you express your true feelings directly, your children will usually calm down. They feel comfortable with the truth, with the congruity between your feelings and your words.

The following exercises may guide you in discovering how your children mirror you. The exercises can encourage you to express your feelings more directly and honestly to your children.

EXERCISE 45

In the first column, describe several "negative" interactions you've had with your child or children lately, or list some of your child's personality traits that bother you. Then in the second column, ask yourself how these items mirror your own internal state. Once you have seen how their actions mirror your feelings, do not use this information to blame yourself or try to change or fix yourself. The gift is often in the seeing. Some examples follow.

NEGATIVE INTERACTIONS	HOW THESE MIRROR YOU
1. *Sally is constantly rebelling.*	*I feel stuck with my responsibilities. Part of me wants to rebel against being such a "good girl," but I never let myself do that.*
2. *Last Monday night, Billy was unhappy and critical of me and his brothers.*	*I've been very down on myself lately.*
3. *My children have been clinging to me recently. They're so needy.*	*I feel like I never get time for myself. I never get my needs met. There's a child in me that needs to be loved, but I'm too busy being strong and competent.*
4. *My children are self-centered and demanding. I feel like they run right over me.*	*I am the "martyr mother," always sacrificing for my kids. I need to honor the part of me that has demands, too, by learning to set boundaries with my kids and say "no" to them when appropriate.*

1.

2.

3.

NEGATIVE INTERACTIONS	HOW THESE MIRROR YOU
4.	
5.	
6.	
7.	
8.	
9.	
10.	

Next list all the positive things you see in your children, and in the second column describe how these, too, mirror you. Examples are given.

POSITIVE INTERACTIONS	HOW THESE MIRROR YOU
1. *My children decide they're going to do something and they do it.*	*I feel comfortable with my children's independence. I like to have time to do what I love to do.*
2. *Rebecca seems to talk easily about how she feels.*	*I have been learning to accept my feelings. I express how I feel with my family.*
3. *John enjoys playing the piano, and gave a recital in school.*	*I was never allowed to be truly creative as a child, but I am learning ways of expressing my creativity now. I am proud of my children's creativity.*

1.

2.

3.

4.

POSITIVE INTERACTIONS	*HOW THESE MIRROR YOU*
5.	
6.	
7.	
8.	
9.	
10.	

EXERCISE 46

Practice telling the truth to your children and expressing your feelings honestly with them even if you feel vulnerable and uncomfortable about not being in control. Ask them how they feel about things and pay close attention to what they have to say. If you are tempted to give advice, ask them if they want to hear it first. If they don't, describe your feelings honestly instead.

Use the space below to record the results of these interactions with your children. Reviewing your notes from time to time will give you a sense of perspective on your evolving relationship with your children. It will also help you identify problem areas that reoccur.

EXERCISE 47

Children have tremendous creativity, if it isn't stifled. They can help us to get back in touch with our own creativity if we let them. This exercise is intended to help you loosen up and have fun, and so be more creative, simply by playing with your children. If you don't have children, "borrow" a child to play with!

Sit down at a clean table with your child. Make sure there is plenty of space for each of you. Put crayons in lots of assorted colors (or you can use your own colored pens) in between you. Have plenty of unlined white paper for each of you. Now, without thinking too much, just start coloring. Pick your favorite colors and just let them move across the page. Don't worry about drawing anything in particular. When you feel you are finished, give the drawing to your child, and take theirs. Now each of you must imitate as best you can what the other drew.

For a variation on this exercise, have your child make a doodle on a piece of paper. Now, you finish the doodle by making something out of it. Then switch.

LIFE AND DEATH

To be alive means to choose to follow the flow of energy within ourselves. Whenever we trust in and live according to the flow of our life energy, our channel expands and fills our physical body with energy. Even our cells are renewed and nourished, so we feel vital and healthy. The more the life force flows through us, the more alive we feel.

Death results when we choose, either consciously or unconsciously, to close down our channel, to block the flow of life energy in our being. When we turn away from following our own inner truth our body suffers from the decreased life force that results. Gradually we deteriorate, physically, emotionally, and spiritually. We all have seen how stress and emotional blockages have taken their toll on us and those around us — a haggard expression, the deep lines of worry etched in the face, constant back pain, and, eventually, serious — even terminal — illness.

The following exercises can help you to become more aware of the direction you are choosing — toward life or toward death — in every aspect of your life. They may help you to make the choice each day to live fully and deeply in the light of renewed vigor and joy.

In the space below, write an ideal scene of how your life would be if you were able to really love and trust yourself and live fully from your own inner sense of truth and integrity. What would it be like to make daily choices that allow you to feel fully alive?

Now, think about and write down the habits, concerns, or fears that keep you from being able to live fully and freely.

EXERCISE 49

In the space below, list the commitment(s) you are willing to make at this moment to choose life. For example:

1. *I am now willing to work four days a week instead of five. I will work less and relax more. This will renew and nourish me.*
2. *I will stop stuffing my feelings. I will find a good therapist who can help me express my feelings.*
3. *I will spend one evening a week working on my creative project.*
4. *One day a month I will commit to following my intuition every moment of that day. I will keep a special journal during that time to record the results of this decision.*

1.

2.

3.

4.

5.

A NEW WAY OF LIFE

W e are living in very exciting and powerful times. Throughout the planet, a radical spiritual transformation is taking place. Every one of us is being challenged to let go of our present way of life and create an entirely new one. We are, in fact, in the process of leaving behind the way of the old world and building a new world in its place.

The old world was based on an external focus. In this world we have continually sought happiness and fulfillment in external things — money, material possessions, relationships, work, fame, good deeds, food, or drugs. But the simple truth is that the old way of life that we have been following for centuries does not work. It has never brought us the deep fulfillment, satisfaction, and joy that we have always sought. And we are now endangering our entire planet. As we awaken to this realization, we are intuitively seeking a conscious connection with the spiritual.

The new world is being established on this spiritual foundation. As each of us connects with our inner spiritual awareness, we also learn that we can create our own reality, and we are beginning to understand how to take responsibility for doing so. The change begins within each individual, but as more and more individuals are transformed, the mass consciousness is increasingly affected.

As we make the transition from the old world to the new, things may appear to be going from bad to worse. It may seem that many things which used to work are not working any more. Actually, things *are* falling apart and will continue to do so with even greater intensity, but this is a positive, natural part of the process of change. We feel upset because we are emotionally attached to following our old way of living. The transition can be exciting if we can open our eyes to the profound changes that are occurring and welcome them.

We are now learning how to live in accordance with the true laws of the universe. Living in harmony with the universe is living totally rich lives, full of vitality, joy, power, love, and abundance on every level. So, although letting go of the old world may be difficult at times, it is well worth whatever it takes to make the transition into the new world. This is a process that cannot be pushed or hurried. We are challenged to appreciate and take with us the valuable aspects of our old way of being while moving, at our own pace, forward into the new. It is a lifelong journey.

The following exercises may help you in making your journey from the old world to the new world with joy and awareness.

EXERCISE 50

MEDITATION

Close your eyes and take a few deep breaths. Let go of any outside concerns and drop into a quiet place within yourself.

Imagine that you are under the stars in a quiet, peaceful place. A huge bonfire rages in front of you. Feel the warmth of the fire and the peacefulness of the air around you. Then slowly begin to move around the fire, and as you do, throw into the fire anything that represents the old way of life for you. Move around the fire saying, "I now release struggle in my life. I now release fear, sickness, or disharmony in my world. I now release and toss into the fire any and all poverty, I now release _____."

(Fill in the blank with as many items as you want.) Keep moving around the fire, letting go of anything that is an old way for you, feeling yourself lighten up as you do.

When you feel you've released whatever you no longer need from your old way of life, walk away from the fire and stand under the stars. Rejoice in the lightness of unburdening yourself.

Imagine yourself opening your arms wide and welcoming in the new. You've created a void by releasing the old so now you can fill that void with the new. Stay open to images of what this newness is. As you receive images of the new, you may want to say, "I now receive ease and joy in my life, I now receive abundance, I now claim a peaceful world, I now receive _____."

(Again, fill in the blank.) Stand there as long as you want, as long as you feel willing to receive and claim the gifts of the universe. When you feel ready, leave the stars and the bonfire and feel yourself come back into the room, refreshed and filled with energy of your new world.

On the next page, list the things you are now willing to release. Then, tear out the page and burn it to symbolize your release of the old.

On the second blank page that follows, list the new things you are now ready to receive. Claim these as yours.

Things I Am Willing To Release

New Things I Am Now Ready To Receive

EXERCISE 51

Describe your new way of life below. Write it in the present tense as if it were already true. What does it look and feel like for you and for the world around you? Spend a few minutes every day visualizing this. As you give the vision more attention, notice how it will gradually start to manifest as a reality in your life.

MAKING CHANGE

———

How can we take action to make positive change in the world? When faced with this challenge, many of us respond in one of the following ways:

1.) We become overwhelmed, feeling that nothing we can do will be of any use, and thus we do nothing. Or,

2.) Driven by conscious or unconscious fear and despair, we adopt a cause or a course of action from a "victim" or "rescuer" position. Then we struggle, fight, or sacrifice to try to "save the world." This way of going about things tends to perpetuate the very problems we're trying to solve.

There is a third alternative. True transformation, on a personal and planetary level, is achieved as more and more of us listen to our own inner guidance and follow our own life flow, thereby fulfilling our life purpose and contributing to the world through our own greatest gifts. As we do what we love, we experience pleasure, excitement, and aliveness and the world is enhanced by our very presence. From this energy, any type of direct social or political action we take is tremendously effective.

These exercises can help you find ways to make effective positive change in the world.

———

EXERCISE 52

MEDITATION

Get in a comfortable position, relax and close your eyes. Breathe slowly and deeply, and as you release each breath, move into a deeper level of relaxation. Bring your awareness into a deep place within, the place where you are connected with your own greatest wisdom. Ask your inner guidance to let you know what your role is in helping to bring positive change into the world. Then sit quietly and be receptive to what comes to you in feelings, words, or images. If you wish, ask for clarification or more specifics. If nothing seems to come, let it go, and know that it will come to you in some form at some time in the near future. Repeat this meditation whenever you wish, as more awareness and information may unfold.

Some examples of awareness that might come through this meditation are:

"I have a natural gift for teaching. I help people learn how to live more fulfilling lives."

"I'm great at organizing and taking care of business. I need to seek a worthy cause that needs my talents, and help them be more successful at what they're trying to do."

"My primary gift is nurturing my children, my friends, myself. As I nurture others I heal and empower them, and when I nurture myself I set a good example for others."

"I have a lot of good ideas about how I'd like to see things done in this city. I'd like to run for city council."

"I'm here to lighten things up. I love to have fun and make people laugh. I just need to keep doing the things that are fun for me, and including other people in my fun."

EXERCISE 53

Write a list of things you enjoy doing that contribute something to the world and/or that could help make positive change in some way, small or large. Include things even if they only affect one or a few other people, or animals, or a small part of the earth.

Every day (or once a week) pick one thing and do it, with full conscious knowledge that you are doing something to bring positive change into this world.

1.

2.

3.

4.

5.

6.

7.

8.

9.

10.

NOTES

NOTES

NOTES

NOTES

NOTES

NOTES

About the Author

Shakti Gawain is the bestselling author of *Creative Visualization, Living in the Light, Return to the Garden, Awakening, Path of Transformation,* and several other books. A warm, articulate, and inspiring teacher, Shakti leads workshops internationally. For nearly twenty years, she has facilitated thousands of people in learning to trust and act on their own inner truth, thus releasing and developing their creativity in every area of their lives.

Shakti and her husband, Jim Burns, are co-founders of Nataraj Publishing. They make their home in Mill Valley, California, and on the island of Kauai.

Also by Shakti Gawain

Books:

Creative Visualization
Creative Visualization Workbook
Living in the Light (with Laurel King)
Living in the Light Workbook
Reflections in the Light: Daily Thoughts and Affirmations
Awakening: A Daily Guide to Conscious Living
Return to the Garden
Meditations
The Path of Transformation

Cassettes:

Creative Visualization
Living in the Light
Developing Intuition
Meditation Series:
   Contacting Your Inner Guide
   The Male and Female Within
   Discovering Your Inner Child
   Expressing Your Creative Being
Relationships As Mirrors
The Path of Transformation

Nataraj Publishing

is committed to acting as a catalyst for change and transformation in the world by providing books and tapes on the leading edge in the fields of personal and social consciousness growth. "Nataraj" is a Sanskrit word referring to the creative, transformative power of the universe. For more information on our company, please contact us at:

Nataraj Publishing
P.O. Box 2430
Mill Valley, CA 94942
Phone: (415) 388-7195

Workshops

Shakti Gawain gives talks and leads workshops all over the United States and in many other countries. She also conducts retreats, intensives, and training programs. If you would like to be on her mailing list and receive workshop information, write or call:

Shakti Gawain, Inc.
P.O. Box 377
Mill Valley, CA 94942
Telephone: (415) 388-7140

Shakti and her husband, Jim Burns, rent rooms and a guest cottage at their beautiful estate on the Hawaiian island of Kauai, for individuals and couples wishing to come for personal retreats. For information or to make reservations, call or write:

Kai Mana
P.O. Box 612
Kilauea, Hawaii 96754
Telephone: (808) 828-1280

Other Books and Tapes from Nataraj Publishing

Books

Living in the Light: A Guide to Personal and Planetary Transformation. By Shakti Gawain, with Laurel King. The recognized classic on developing intuition and using it as a guide in living your life. (Tradepaper $11.95)

Living in the Light Workbook. By Shakti Gawain. Following up her bestseller, *Living in the Light,* Shakti has created a workbook to help us apply these principles to our lives in very practical ways. (Tradepaper $12.95)

Return to the Garden: A Journey of Discovery. By Shakti Gawain. Shakti reveals her path to self-discovery and personal power and shows us how to return to our personal garden and live on earth in a natural and balanced way. (Tradepaper $11.95)

Awakening: A Daily Guide to Conscious Living. By Shakti Gawain. A daily meditation guide that focuses on maintaining your spiritual center, not just when you are in solitude, but when you are in the world, and especially, in relationships. (Tradepaper $9.95)

Embracing Our Selves: The Voice Dialogue Manual. By Drs. Hal and Sidra Stone. The highly acclaimed, groundbreaking work that explains the psychology of the selves and the Voice Dialogue method. (Tradepaper $12.95)

Embracing Each Other: Relationship as Teacher, Healer and Guide. By Drs. Hal and Sidra Stone. A compassionate guide to understanding and improving our relationships. The follow-up to the Stone's pioneering book on Voice Dialogue. (Tradepaper $11.95)
Maps to Ecstasy: Teachings of an Urban Shaman. By Gabrielle Roth, with John Loudon. A modern shaman shows us how to reconnect to the vital energetic core of our being through dance, song, theater, writing, meditation, and ritual. (Tradepaper $10.95)

Notes from My Inner Child: I'm Always Here. By Tanha Luvaas. This deeply touching book puts us in contact with the tremendous energy and creativity of the inner child. (Tradepaper $8.95)

Coming Home: The Return to True Self. By Martia Nelson. A down-to-earth spiritual primer that explains how we can use the very flaws of our humanness to carry the vibrant energy of our true self and reach the potential that dwells in all of us. (Tradepaper $12.95)

Corporate Renaissance: Business as an Adventure in Human Development. By Rolf Osterberg. This groundbreaking book explodes the myth that a business's greatest asset is capital, and shows how employees must come first for businesses to succeed in the '90s. (Hardcover $18.95)

Passion to Heal: The Ultimate Guide to Your Healing Journey. By Echo Bodine. An invaluable guide for mapping out our individual journeys to health. (Tradepaper $14.95)

The Path of Transformation: How Healing Ourselves Can Change the World. By Shakti Gawain. Shakti gave us *Creative Visualization* in the '70s, *Living in the Light* in the '80s, and now *The Path of Transformation* for the '90s. Shakti's new bestseller delivers an inspiring and provocative message for the path of true transformation. (Tradepaper $11.95)

The Revelation: A Message of Hope for the New Millennium. By Barbara Marx Hubbard. An underground classic from one of the true prophets of our time. Hubbard offers an astonishing interpretation of the Book of Revelation, which reveals the consciousness required by the human race, not only to survive, but to blossom into full realization of its potential. (Tradepaper $16.95)

The Shadow in America: Reclaiming the Soul of a Nation. Edited by Jeremiah Abrams. Ten visionaries, including bestselling authors Thomas Moore and Robert Bly, discuss our nation's shadow and its role in gender relations, racism, politics, sexuality, addiction, and love. (Tradepaper $12.95)

Awakening the Warrior Within. By Dawn Callan. This book explodes contemporary myths about attaining personal safety, revealing how they may actually contribute to our victimization, and introduces the Warrior Code—ten important keys for making the journey back to power. (Tradepaper $12.95)

The Turtle Tattoo: Timeless Tales for Finding and Fulfilling Your Dreams. By Margaret Olivia Wolfson. The author has gathered together allegories and tales that have moved people to achieve happiness and success for centuries. She lays out a powerful 11-step plan for achieving success on any path we might choose. (Hardcover $14.95)

AUDIOCASSETTES

Living in the Light: Read by Shakti Gawain. Shakti reads her bestseller on developing intuition. (Two-tape set $15.95)

Developing Intuition. Shakti Gawain expands on the ideas about intuition that she first discussed in *Living in the Light.* (One audiocassette $10.95)

The Path of Transformation: How Healing Ourselves Can Change the World. Read by Shakti Gawain. Shakti's bestseller on audiocassette. (Two-tape set $15.95)

The Four Levels of Healing. From the Journey to Wholeness series, Shakti Gawain's empowering two-tape set offers compelling evidence that it is only through healing on physical, emotional, mental, and spiritual levels that we may become whole! (Two-tape set $14.95)

Nataraj Publishing is committed to acting as a catalyst for change and transformation in the world by providing books and audiocassettes on the leading edge in the fields of personal and social consciousness growth. *Nataraj* is a Sanskrit word referring to the creative, transformative power of the universe. For more information on our company, please contact us at: **Nataraj Publishing, P.O. Box 2430, Mill Valley, CA 94942**

To Place an Order: Call (800) 949-1091.